This document
as a statement
and Mistresses
AMMA changed
Association of 1
(ATL) on 1 January 1993.

CONTENTS   *Page*

References in the text to works cited in the Bibliography are marked [ ].

Chapter 1

Introduction: the debate so far

The public debate about multi-cultural education has been going on for a long time, possibly ever since the Notting Hill race riots of 1958. The first official recognition that the large numbers of recent immigrants produced a need for changes in provisions of public services, including education, came in Section 11 of the 1966 Local Government Act [1]. This was followed by the 1968 and 1976 Race Relations Acts [2,3].

In 1969 the Select Committee on Race Relations and Immigration turned its attention specifically to education with its report *The problems of coloured school leavers [4]*. In 1977 the Government's Green Paper *Education in schools: a consultative document [5]* said:

"Our country is a multi-cultural, multi-racial one, and the curriculum should reflect a sympathetic understanding of different cultures and races that now make up society."

In the same year the Select Committee report, *The West Indian community [6]*, pointed out widespread concern about the poor performance in British schools of children of West Indian origin. It was partly as a result of this report that a committee of inquiry was established in 1979 under the chairmanship first of Mr Anthony Rampton and later of Lord Swann. The terms of reference of the inquiry were:

"Recognising the contribution of schools in preparing all pupils for life in a society which is both multi-racial and culturally diverse, the Committee is required to:

review in relation to schools the educational needs and attainments of children from ethnic minority groups taking account, as necessary, of factors outside the formal education system relevant to school performance, including influences in early childhood and prospects for school leavers;

consider the potential value of instituting arrangements for keeping under review the educational performance of different ethnic minority groups, and what those arrangements might be; consider the most effective use of resources for these purposes; and to make recommendations." *[9], page 1*

The creation of this committee did much to accelerate the pace of debate on multi-cultural education, including much valuable work by the Schools Council. It was at this stage that AMMA published its first booklet on the subject, *Education for a multi-cultural society [7]*, which was the text of its submission to the Rampton Committee.

The year 1981 saw riots in Brixton and other areas and the setting up of an inquiry under the chairmanship of Lord Scarman. The report of this *[8]* was published in November 1981, five months after the Rampton interim report *West Indian children in our schools [9]* and soon after a report of the Select Committee on Home Affairs about *Racial disadvantage [10]*. The last of the group of reports to appear at this time was *The secondary school curriculum and examinations [11]* from the House of Commons Education, Science and the Arts Committee in 1982.

The selections of these four reports dealing with, or touching on, education for a multi-cultural society had much common ground in arguing for a multi-cultural focus to the curriculum for all pupils, minority and majority alike. This was a point which had been central to AMMA's evidence to Rampton and which was developed further in an AMMA publication of 1983, *Our multi-cultural society: the educational response [12]*. This booklet, which among other things responded to the four reports, was launched at a one-day conference. It took as its central theme the need to offer pupils and students an education that would equip them with the skills they would need in daily life (including a command of standard English) and also enable them to make a considered choice of life-style drawing on elements of the majority native culture and their own ancestral culture as they themselves wished. A multi-cultural curriculum, we argued, would work towards this and would also lay foundations for a fairer society in which racial and cultural diversity was seen as having positive value.

The Rampton Report was not followed by much action by Government to implement its recommendations and it was felt by some to be significant that fairly soon afterwards Mr Rampton resigned the chairmanship of the Committee, to be succeeded by Lord Swann.

At this time the public debate began to develop a new flavour. Rampton had talked about unintentional racism and from then on the word racism moved much nearer the centre of the debate. Fears, long-held by many people in ethnic-minority groups, that their educational progress was being seriously hampered by racism became much more clearly and publicly articulated. Some black groups expressed the view that a multi-cultural approach to the curriculum offered little or nothing towards solving their problems in comparison with more directly anti-racist teaching. The use of the word racism in the public debate has not always been consistent, and the stridency of its use by some participants has not been helpful. The concept of racism is the subject of our Chapter 2.

The intensified level of debate prompted by the four reports did produce positive responses from some parts of the education service. Rather more LEAs than had previously done so began taking the issues seriously, as can be evidenced in the growth since that time of the number of LEA officers and advisers with designated responsibilities in the field of multi-cultural or anti-racist education, and the increasing number of LEAs and individual schools which were prompted to produce policy documents on the subject. Examination boards also began to react much more positively than previously to questions raised by the multi-cultural nature of their clientele and of society as a whole, questions which many teachers had previously accused the boards of ignoring..

The long-awaited Swann report, *Education for all [13]*, was published in March 1985 at a length of 807 pages. It took a strong multi-culturalist line about the curriculum, which revived debate about the rival merits of "multi-cultural" and "anti-racist" approaches. Its Chapter 2, "Racism: Theory and Practice", said much of value that we comment on later. It is to be regretted that this chapter was not referred to in Lord Swann's "brief guide" to the report [14], thus leading many people to believe the report to have said nothing about racism. Taken in conjunction with some other sections of the report considering the three-way link between ethnic minority membership, socio-economic class and educational attainment, this led to criticism from some quarters that Swann "blamed everything on the home background".

When the publication of the report was announced in Parliament by the Secretary of State [15], he said that action would be taken on three fronts:

✳ to improve standards in schools for all pupils,
✳ to tackle the obstacles that prevent ethnic minority pupils having the same opportunities as others,
✳ to make sure that schools preserve and transmit national values in a way which accepts Britain's ethnic diversity and promotes tolerance and racial harmony.

He explicitly rejected four of Swann's recommendations:

✳ a review of the statutory requirement for a daily corporate act of worship in maintained schools,
✳ a review of the legal distinction between county and voluntary schools,
✳ an extension of mandatory grants to cover special access courses in preparation for higher education,
✳ amendment of Section 11 of the 1966 Local Government Act.

Shortly afterwards he set up a working party at the DES to look at the possible value and practicability of collecting statistics (at either national or LEA level) about the ethnic composition of the school pupil population. This had been recommended in the Rampton Report and echoed by Swann. The main recommendations of this group were accepted by the Secretary of State in a statement to the House of Commons in 1986 [16]. They will be discussed in Chapter 8.

As this group was nearing the end of its work, the DES embarked on a consultation process about increasing the supply of teachers from ethnic minorities. At the same time another working party was set up to consider collecting ethnic statistics about teachers and about student teachers in training. This happened in a context where, prompted perhaps by the publication of the Community Relations Commission's code of practice for employers, a number of LEAs had begun, with varying degrees of consultation, to collect such information in an attempt to monitor the ethnic composition of their work-force.

The debate continues. Understanding of the nature and purpose of a multi-cultural curriculum is much more widespread than it was a few years ago. Practice lags some way behind the official recognition of the need.

Regrettably, some people still feel that a multi-cultural approach is irrelevant to their mono-cultural school. This attitude is becoming less prevalent as more and more parts of the country find themselves with ethnic minority populations as a result of increased mobility.

Some still reject the multi-cultural curriculum as irrelevant to the target of eradicating racism. This view we reject. It is true that a multi-cultural curriculum does not always have a short-term effect on the practice of racism and that other short-term strategies are therefore needed. But the long-term target of creating a society free from racism has to involve as a central weapon the education of future citizens to see cultural diversity as a positive thing, to welcome and understand it. This is what the multi-cultural curriculum is about. Anti-racism seeks to cure and multi-cultural education to prevent the exercise of racial prejudice.

There is much in society, and in the education service in particular, which operates to the disadvantage of people from ethnic minorities. The extent to which it is useful to use the label "racism" is open to debate. There are some people who have been deterred from addressing the issues by the stridency of some advocates of so doing. This is most unfortunate since the issues are real and will not go away. If we are to achieve a society, and an education system, with a true equality of opportunity then the issues frequently bundled together as "racism" need to be tackled, and tackled urgently.

One other change that has come over the debate recently is a growing awareness of the close links between questions of equal opportunity for people of different ethnic groups and those of

8

equal opportunity for men and women. The fundamental questions are the same. Both sets of questions involve tackling prejudices based on considering people as members of groups rather than as individuals. In both aspects prejudicial opinion can lead to discriminatory behaviour. More and more people and organisations active in one field are finding themselves involved in the other. But at times the two can find themselves opposed as, for example, in questions concerning the education of girls from some Asian cultures.

This is the context in which we have written this booklet and the reason why discussion of racism, prejudice and equal opportunity will form the focus of its thought.

Our central thesis remains unchanged from our earlier booklet and is very much in tune with the main thrust of the Swann Report. We believe that a broad multi-cultural curriculum for all pupils, irrespective of their racial, cultural and linguistic backgrounds, is the prime means by which education can contribute to the elimination of racial injustice from society. All, not least the white majority, need to be led to an understanding of the cultural diversity to be found in Britain today, and to view this diversity in a positive light.

All pupils need an education that will equip them with the tools necessary for daily life: for pupils from linguistic minorities this is particularly important in the area of English, but help here must not be at the expense of devaluing their home language. We examine questions of language in Chapter 3.

One of the arguments on this point in our previous publication was later quoted approvingly in the Swann Report:

"Pupils from all backgrounds will one day be voting, decision-making citizens whose views will influence public policies which affect people of all cultural backgrounds. All will contribute to the values of society. It is therefore important that all are made aware of the multi-cultural nature of British society today, and are encouraged in the attitudes of mutual knowledge and toleration which alone can make such a multi-cultural society a fair and successful one."

[12] page 15, quoted in [13] page 319

9

People whose ancestral culture is different from that of the majority group among whom they live are faced with difficult decisions. To what extent should they maintain their separateness? How far should they submerge their cultural origins in an attempt to integrate with the host culture in order to succeed in it? What compromise between these two options is right for each of them as an individual? These questions are faced no less by ethnic minority youngsters born and brought up in this country than by first-generation immigrants. Indeed the lack of first-hand knowledge of the family's country of origin can make the question of identity sharper than ever.

We believe that a multi-cultural education for all pupils will eventually make these questions easier if it results in a society where positive acceptance of diversity becomes increasingly the norm. For the individuals themselves, such a programme will also enable them to face these choices from a position of greater knowledge and to make better-informed choices. This we think is of central importance. Our views on the necessary multi-cultural nature of the curriculum are set out in Chapter 4.

The curriculum at secondary level and above has a complex interaction with the examination system. While in an ideal world the curriculum should lead the examinations, too often the reality seems to be the other way round. At one time the examination system seemed to provide a straitjacket limiting the extent that secondary schools could move towards a multi-cultural curriculum. Recent changes of attitude on the part of many exam boards, thankfully in time to have an effect on the development of the GCSE, have made the picture rather healthier in this respect. Multi-cultural considerations for the examination system are the subject of Chapter 5.

Schools do not exist in isolation. Each is part of a wider local community. School pupils go on to further education, to employment, to training or to the dole. The way in which these links happen needs to take into account the multi-cultural nature of society. This, together with the vexed question of separate schools, forms the subject of Chapter 6.

The education process depends on teachers. If their training, both initial and in-service, does not keep pace with developments in educational thinking, then there is little hope that those developments can be effective. Teachers who are themselves members of ethnic minorities have an important part to play, as role-models as well as directly as teachers. It is a commonplace that there are not enough such people. This situation is not only an injustice to the minority groups, but a limitation on the effectiveness of the education service. Questions of teacher education and recruitment are the subject of Chapter 7.

We acknowledge that many of the aims we describe, and the means we propose of achieving them, are long-term. They need to be accompanied by effective and well considered short-term measures to offset the very real and immediate racism that exists in society today. Since our previous publication we have concluded that this aspect requires more emphasis than we gave it at that time. Chapter 8 examines what can be done.

Chapter 2

What do we mean by racism?

In the previous chapter we noted that in recent years the word 'racism' has moved much nearer the centre of the debate about education in a multi-cultural society. The word is one which has been used variously in different contexts and for different purposes. It is the purpose of this chapter to examine some of these uses and suggest which of them are useful.

Many writers and speakers have used the word loosely without precise definition, and this has, to some extent, brought about a debasement of its proper use and a rejection of the whole debate on the part of those people who are put off by what they see as strident sloganising. Our previous publication said on this point:

"There are certain attitudes and practices, in no way racist in intent, which have an unintended (and often unrealised) adverse effect on the opportunities for members of minority ethnic groups. To identify these as 'racist' can often be an accurate description of the effects perceived by the minority groups who suffer from them. To go further and to subject these attitudes and practices to the same vilification as overt and intentional racism is not a technique that is likely to have a persuasive effect on their practitioners. It is more likely to alienate them than to change their practice for the better."

[12] page 14

In a recent article Peter Newsam (chairman of the Community Relations Commission and a former education officer of ILEA) states the problem and suggests an answer:

"Over-emphasising a single principle becomes explosive when terms like 'racist' are added to the debate. The term racist hurled at an opponent usually has the intellectual content and much the same effect as a custard pie. Here then is a definition of 'racism' intended to cause pie-slingers to pause, pie poised: whereas to teach everyone badly is merely incompetent, to teach in ways that disproportionately disadvantage ethnic minorities is racist.

"So to dodge the issue of racial injustice in all-white schools may be racist because it disproportionately disadvantages black youths when some of those untaught white youngsters later become employers, football fans, union officials or join the police. Similarly, disproportionately to fail to enable ethnic minority youngsters to enter society on equal terms, by neglecting to teach them to read properly, may be racist, and so on."

[17]

Prejudice against people who are different from oneself is, regrettably, a common phenomenon and racial prejudice is just one of its forms. Racial prejudice is not restricted to views held by white people about black people. It can occur the other way round, or between sub-divisions of the white and black groups. Such prejudice is hard to eliminate: possibly it can be eliminated only by a long-term educational strategy over more than one generation: hence our continuing support for a multi-cultural curriculum for all.

It is when this emotional prejudice extends to discriminatory behaviour that the result may merit the term 'racism'. For this to happen requires that the prejudiced person or group has to be in a position of sufficient power to exercise discrimination. This is why, in Britain today, prejudice held by white people about black people is more dangerous in practice than the reverse prejudice.

By and large the majority population has more access than the ethnic minorities to the reins of power that can be used to turn prejudice into discrimination. The reasons for this are rooted in our colonial past, including the way in which, during the period immediately following the Second World War, Britain attempted to solve its problem of shortage of labour by encouraging widespread immigration from what is now called the New Commonwealth. The new arrivals were relegated to the most menial tasks which were not congenial to the indigenous population. This set up a whole complex of attitudes and socio-economic conditions, much of which remains with us today.

This is the justification for a widely used definition of racism which combines simplicity with accurate analysis:

PREJUDICE + POWER = RACISM

The word "power" in this equation is capable of different interpretations to fit different circumstances. In considerations of society as a whole it is political and economic power which are relevant, both strongly concentrated in the hands of the ethnic majority. Within the education service, whether at national, LEA or school level, the relevant power is that of the hierarchy, again dominantly from the ethnic majority. But in a more localised context, such as an individual class in a school, the relevant power may well be the social power of the peer-group which can, in some circumstances, make black racism a very real thing.

But not all forms of discriminatory behaviour are rooted in individual prejudice, whether deliberate or subconscious. The Rampton Report made much of what it called "unintentional racism", a similar concept to what is often called "institutional racism":

"The suggestion that teachers are in any way racist understandably arouses very strong reactions from the profession and is often simply rejected out of hand as entirely unjustified and malicious.

"Since a profession of nearly half a million people must to a great extent reflect the attitudes of society at large there must inevitably be some teachers who hold explicitly racist views. Such teachers are very much in the minority. We have, however, found some evidence of what we have described as unintentional racism in the behaviour and attitudes of other teachers whom it would be misleading to describe as racist in the commonly accepted sense. They firmly believe that any prejudices they may have can do no harm since they are not translated into openly discriminatory behaviour. Nevertheless, if their attitudes are influenced in any way by prejudices against ethnic minority groups, this can and does, we believe, have a detrimental effect on all children whom they encounter."

[9] page 12

Racism, in the sense of discriminatory practice, is certainly a major part of the black experience, taking "black" in its widest, most inclusive sense. What is experienced here is racism defined

14

by effect, some of which, but only some, is also racism defined by intention.

An alternative, and in our view better, definition of institutional racism, comes from an ILEA policy statement:

"Other forms of discrimination are less easy to perceive but are equally important. They include procedures employed within the education service, in its administration as well as in its institutions, which, however well-intended or rooted in custom, may have the effect of reducing the opportunities open to members of minority ethnic groups. These procedures need to be re-examined. Similarly deep-seated attitudes adversely affecting members of minority ethnic groups are widespread. These attitudes need to be brought to the surface and challenged."

[18]

A good example of institutional racism is quoted in Chapter 7, concerning the way advertisement of posts and hidden assumptions by interviewers about what is "normal" can hamper the employment prospects of people from minority groups.

The Swann Report has been unjustly criticised for ignoring the question of racism. In fact its Chapter 2, 'Racism: theory and practice' gives detailed discussion of the topic. As we said before, the low level of public awareness of this excellent chapter is possibly connected with the omission of any reference to it in Lord Swann's "brief guide" to the Report [14]. Whatever the reason, we feel that this chapter has not received the attention it deserves and so make no apology for rehearsing its main arguments here.

It begins with a brief discussion of prejudice in general:

"Because prejudice in its very nature often overlooks the actual qualities and merits of an individual person, it is often directed against (and, less frequently, in favour of) groups of people who are assumed to share common attributes and behaviour patterns. Prejudice thus requires that one has formed a stereotype of a particular 'group' of people, be they women drivers, trade unionists or 'immigrants', which then allows one to judge a member of this group, and in particular their actions, according to an established set of expectations...

"The role of education in relation to prejudice is surely

15

therefore clear – to equip a pupil with knowledge and understanding in place of ignorance and to develop his or her ability to formulate views and attitudes and to assess and judge situations on the basis of knowledge."

[13] pages 12-13

The chapter goes on to discuss "the ethnic-minority dimension of prejudice" as exemplified by the widespread description of all ethnic minorities as "immigrants" and "foreigners" despite the fact that the overwhelming majority of ethnic-minority children in Britain today were born here. There is discussion of the prevalence of crude stereotypes of minority groups, fuelled by ignorance and the influence of the media.

"A further dimension which we found in our visits to 'all white' areas – which clearly illustrates the irrationality of some aspects of racism – is the confusion which can arise where there are *conflicting* stereotypes, for example, where youngsters from the majority community may be prejudiced against Asians on the grounds that, on the one hand, 'they all live on Social Security', and on the other, that 'they're all taking our jobs'."

[13] page 17

The chapter goes on to examine the roots of racism in the history of immigration into Britain, in some cases a drive to escape from persecution elsewhere, in others a search for economic betterment, sometimes actively encouraged by British Governments or employers in times of economic growth. In most cases the groups concerned were initially welcomed but this attiude was reversed when an economic down-swing changed the employment market at a time when many of the minority groups (often the children of the original immigrants) were aspiring to higher-status jobs than the ones at the lower end of the market to which the original immigrants had been confined.

Swann examines the expectations that different minority communities have held of Britain when they first came, pointing out that certain fallacies have frequently arisen.

The "myth of an alternative", common among European minorities and the Hong Kong Chinese, is that if they fail to find employment in Britain they can always return to their country of origin. In practice they may well be no more welcome there.

The "myth of return", common in some Asian communities, that their stay in Britain is purely temporary, persists despite the changed reality that comes when a subsequent generation is British-born. We refer again to this point in Chapter 6.

The "myth of belonging", that they really are British in a strong sense, was probably at its strongest among the original immigrants from the West Indies – Christian, English-speaking, brought up in a British-style education system focused on British culture. It is perhaps people with this expectation that have found it hardest to come to terms with the real prejudice and discrimination they have met. The Report quotes a West Indian mother:

"Many of us came here with a myth in our minds, the myth of belonging. We have also raised our children to believe that they belong in these societies and cultures (simply because they were born here) only to find that as they grew older, they were seen in the eyes of the host community as a new nation of intruders. Our children are then faced with great traumatic and psychological problems, since they are made to feel that they do not belong here, also they feel that because they were not born in the West Indies they do not belong there either ..."

[13] page 21

At one time the Department of Education and Science used to collect statistics of the numbers of immigrant children in schools. The definition of "immigrant" for this purpose was a child born outside the UK who had been resident here for less than ten years. The hidden assumption in this was that after about ten years an immigrant family would have been assimilated into British society and be, for all educational purposes, indistinguishable from the majority group. One of the factors that led to the end of this type of analysis was the realisation by many teachers that not only was the hidden assumption false as a description of reality, but that it did not even describe the aspirations of many cultural minority groups.

We believe that the reality is better described by the word "accommodation", seen as a dual purpose. The newcomers need

17

to make certain adjustments in their way of life and (most particularly) their language in order to function effectively in the everyday life of their host country; in turn the host population makes some changes in its customs and culture. This mutual adjustment has begun to occur more widely than many recognise, particularly in areas where cultural minorities are present in significant numbers. Such accommodation, based upon mutual toleration and respect, seems to us to be a natural and healthy process to be encouraged. It should not be opposed in the pursuit of a concept of integration if this is to be achieved by pressure upon minority groups to abandon their cultural inheritance and sense of identity.

The next section of the report deals with racism in practice within the education system. It finds widespread stereotyping and ethnocentrism among teachers, confirming, in particular, the earlier findings in the Rampton Report of widespread low academic expectations of West Indian children. It suggests that Asian children, on the other hand, are seen through a more positive educational stereotype but are more likely to suffer direct racial harassment and attack.

One traditional liberal view comes under attack in the report:

"...it is clear that there is a substantial body of opinion within the teaching profession which firmly believes that to recognise differences between people of various ethnic origins is divisive and can in fact constitute a major obstacle to creating a harmonious multi-racial society. We ourselves regard "colour-blindness" however as potentially just as negative as a straightforward rejection of people with a different skin colour since both types of attitude seek to deny the validity of an important aspect of a person"s identity."

[13] pages 26-27

A colour-blind approach by teachers can also lead to cultural impoverishment for their classes since the educational opportunities to be found in the multi-cultural classroom will be missed.

The argument that only white racism needs to be addressed is dismissed, the report setting its face against all prejudice by one group against another. It does, however, acknowledge that the much greater access to power that is open to the majority community puts its prejudices in a position where they can do the most harm.

Institutional racism is examined, in a way similar to the one we have adopted above, and the importance of the wider social context of what takes place in the classroom is stressed:

"In considering the influence which racism whether intentional or unintentional can have on the education process we feel that it is essential to recognise the very direct and acute bearing which the general "climate" of racism in this country has on what takes place in the school classroom. By this we mean the way in which the confidence of ethnic minority groups to see themselves as an integral part of our society and thus having equal claim to shaping their own futures within it, has been undermined and to some extent lost entirely...

"There are two other aspects of the pressures to which ethnic minority communities find themselves subject, which have been raised with us by parents and young people, particularly from the Asian community, and which have undoubtedly contributed greatly to the overall climate of racism: the fear of racial harassment and attack, and the uncertainty created by the policies of successive Governments on immigration and nationality."

[13] pages 30-31

The report quotes the 1981 Home Office report, *Racial attacks,* both as evidence of the prevalence of racial harassment and attacks, major and minor, and also on the role of the media whose sensational reporting of racial incidents raises consciousness of them not only among local communities but also in ethnic minority groups elsewhere.

"A single television interview with a prominent public figure who puts forward a view which appears hostile to the ethnic minority communities can, in its impact, be out of proportion to its significance, and can unreasonably create the impression that that view is held by the authorities generally."

[19] quoted in [13] page 32

The concluding sections of Swann's Chapter 2 consider the

impact of racism on schools and the role of the school. Ethnic minority pupils often see their school as at best oblivious to, at worst conniving in, the racism they experience outside. Swann points out that in this context for a school to seek to remain neutral and uninvolved is effectively to condone racial prejudice and discrimination and to make it difficult for pupils from ethnic minorities to identify with the school community.

Racist abuse – name-calling and graffiti – has a large role in the perception of the school community by pupils from ethnic minorities. Hence, Swann argues, the importance to be placed in schools in dealing with this. We shall pursue this point in Chapter 8.

The chapter finishes by pointing to evidence that racist attitudes are not confined to areas with racially diverse populations. In all-white areas, while racism has less direct opportunity for being put into immediate practice, by the same token there is less immediate evidence to challenge the popular and media stereotypes. The lack of so many schools in such areas to take up the issue and challenge the stereotype contributes to the overall national climate to racism.

We finish our chapter by returning to the article by Peter Newsam which we quoted earlier:

"...the education schools offer does not take place in a moral or political vacuum. The curriculum, defined as all the intended outcomes of the school, has therefore to reflect this.

"...it follows that all schools should exemplify and seek to inculcate certain universally-accepted values. At least since Plato, the notion of justice is one such value. We are in favour of justice, are we not? Conversely, we are against injustice, of which racial injustice in an instance. So there is no room for pussy-footing. The need to eliminate racial injustice should be an integral part of the school curriculum from Cornwall or Cumbria to all inner-cities."

[17]

Chapter 3

Language

"Do you know what language is – it's words – it's bridges – so that you can get safely from one place to another, and the more bridges you know about the more places you can see."

[20]

General principles

There should be no need for us to stress the importance of helping all children to acquire and develop language skills, nor should we need to emphasize the challenge that this presents to all teachers. Since our last publication, however, the circumstances in which we consider the question of language teaching have altered: we have seen HMI's *English from 5 to 16 [21]*, but probably more far-reaching in its influence on secondary teachers has been the fundamental thinking going on in connection with GCSE syllabuses and their implementation. During the same period new emphases have also been emerging in the debate about the most controversial multi-cultural issues in the language field.

The thinking-out of policies must take account not only of awkward paradoxes but also of a far greater degree of sophistication in the discussion. Lord Scarman, like so many others, looked to language teaching to make a decisive contribution to alleviating the worst crises in our society. He wrote:

"The problems which have to be solved if deprivation and alienation are to be overcome, have been identified – namely teaching a command of the English language, a broad education in the humanities designed to help various ethnic groups (including the 'host community') to understand each other's background and culture."

We ourselves must now explain how new perspectives have changed some of our thinking in AMMA and made us revise certain of our previous recommendations about the ways in which we should go about doing this.

We have seen – and we acknowledge – the point made with quiet insistence in the opening section of Chapter 5 of the Swann Report:

"There is now a great diversity of languages spoken among *British* families in *British* homes."

[13] page 385

We may no longer concentrate our thinking mainly on immigrants arriving in a host community. There is also wisdom in Swann's warning that approaches in the past have been hindered by too frequent stressing of language education in a multi-cultural society in terms of the separate "problem" of teaching English to children for whom it is not a first language. We acknowledge there may well have been patronage in the past; we recognise the right asserted by Alladina and others that

"... the multi-lingual communities must be involved in defining the needs, approaches and developing strategies for our children's language education."

[22]

But many voices are raised, often advocating directly opposed programmes. Some difficult choices must therefore be made in good faith to allow purposeful action to be taken; and, if we recognise how paradoxical the situation can be, we know that implementation of policies must be sensitive, holding a variety of considerations in balance. There must also be available greater expertise, better resourced, to effect the improvements we look for.

It is true that the traces linger in society from an earlier tradition of defining children as problems. Yet they must be helped if, as Dr Ashton Gibson's study [23] sets out to show, teachers are still "blinkered" to "the unequal struggle" for which language difficulties are partly responsible, and parents put great pressure on their children as they seek simple solutions. Some of these are the parents who want children "to receive more English, especially grammar teaching, because that is what you need to get on in this society". On the other hand, there are the supporters of the campaign for greater study of Creole in school as "the legitimate language of many pupils" in a society where "whites dictate what blacks want". To whom then should we listen?

Finally, there can certainly be too much stress put on the "deficiency mode" with a consequent growth of negative stereotypes in the minds of teachers and pupils. We agree with the comment in the Swann Report that we should see "diversity and strangeness as sources of interest and stimulus rather than fear and threat". This fits well with the dominant philosophy emerging in the new GCSE syllabuses which put quite as much stress on the need for differentiation in teaching as on standardisation in assessment because of the concern to achieve the maximum development for every pupil.

For these reasons we welcome the starting point from which the Swann Report develops its concept of language and language education (*[13] Chapter 5*). It rightly sees concern for the language development of children from ethnic-minority communities within the larger framework of a much more fully-developed concept of language education for all children.

Nevertheless, there are some particular questions to be considered which are different for the pupils of minority groups from those of the majority.

We recognise three categories of such pupils who have specific language needs:

(i) Some children still arrive in this country knowing little or no English. While for some of the minority communities the period of primary immigration seems to have come to an end, others continue with secondary immigration (the arrival in this country of families to join relatives who have been here for some time), while yet other groups are only just beginning to arrive. Numbers fluctuate and political instability in different parts of the world can often produce a wave of migration to this country as, for example, when Asian families were being expelled from certain African countries.

(ii) Many children, albeit born in this country, experience English as a language used outside the home but never or rarely within it. They will be able to gain the undeniable benefits of bilingualism but there is an inevitable cost in learning to cope with the considerable intellectual and psychological demands which the acquiring of that facility presents.

(iii) Yet others speak English as their first language, but with pronunciation, grammatical structures, vocabulary and speech rhythms which diverge sharply from what, with all its variations, is called Standard English. The language learned from their peer-group will, in all probability, be limited in register.

In Chapter 1 we considered the self-identification questions facing members of ethnic minorities. The home language plays a central role in the all-important view a person takes of his own cultural identity. It is therefore vital that each child's home language is recognised and respected, and that this recognition and respect is made evident through the child's educational experience. This applies to children in all the categories we defined above. The Rampton Report said at one point:

"Teachers who reject a West Indian child's language as inadequate or simply bad English are likely to be those who have not had the opportunity to learn about the nature of West Indian language and are unable to recognise Creole features and cannot therefore react positively and constructively to them. They are likely to regard West Indian pupils as needing remedial language help which may be inappropriate or unnecessary. As far as the 'dialect interference' view is concerned, it is important to remember that by far the majority of West Indian children were born in this country and can use both West Indian Creole and Standard English. They need to be helped to understand clearly the differences and similarities between these two language forms, their relative values in different contexts, and the uses to which they should be put. We would therefore strongly support the 'repertoire' approach to language as one which values and uses all the language forms which all the children bring to school. It enhances the child's self-respect and self-confidence and understanding and appreciation of the nature of language and its different forms and not least of course the development of writing and comprehension skills."

[91] pages 24–25

We fully support this view and consider that, *mutatis mutandis*, it applies much more widely that in its original context of West Indian pupils.

We know that the experience of some members of the minority communities has led them to feel that only by adhering exclusively to a particular form of English developed within their own group may they be loyal to that group and be prepared to proclaim their readiness to promote its concerns. In this view they have sometimes been joined by teachers and others outside the group who wished sincerely to show their respect and support on humanitarian grounds. This attitude to language is not, of course, confined only to groups in the ethnic minority communities. It has always been one important factor which teachers had to take into account in helping many other pupils from different geographical and socio-economic groups who felt their use of language was a vital aspect of their self-identification. Those children always found it hard to determine how far it was right and how far they were willing to adapt their spoken and written expression in contacts with wider audiences in the course of their education and later lives.

On the other hand the requirement of an effective command of English to compete in the search for employment has caused some parents and teachers to show an over-anxious respect for Standard or "correct" English which is so exaggerated that it militates against the pupil's self-image and, by its narrowness, gets in the way of the full maturing of the child's mental and emotional development. It has led to parents" pressing for the very exercises in isolated mechanical skills which HMI, in *English from 5 to 16 [21]*, has pointed out will leave overall comprehension still undeveloped. Pupils are given an exaggerated belief in the value of rote-learning, and grammar on its own is mentioned as the key to more advanced and acceptable communication. HMI pleaded for activities which allow the "purposeful use of language" to develop skills at the deeper levels. If this is the aim, then establishing an early command of idiomatic English through the infants' all-important play activities, and varied practice of written and spoken language in the different registers will surely play a part. In such cases schools may well find they have to persuade parents to adopt a wider view in the interests of their children's real needs.

After long and thorough consideration of all these factors, AMMA has felt bound to take a firm stand on two equally important principles which are applicable to all the groups described above. These principles are:

(a) the need to respect and value the pupil's home language, but equally

(b) the need to facilitate development of an effective command of English for a range of private and public purposes.

If pupils from minority groups are to enjoy the same curricular opportunities at school, and the same employment and citizenship opportunities in later life, then they need to be able to operate effectively within the medium of English as well as developing their range continuously in their mother tongue. In saying this we include most decidedly the more formal registers of Standard English when these are appropriate. If we fail to ensure this for them then they are in danger of becoming confined to a ghetto existence or of being treated to what we assume would be a most unwelcome patronage and indulgence. We agree with the weight of opinion in the Swann Report that

"... essential to equality of opportunity, to academic success and, more broadly, to participation on equal terms as a full member of society is a good command of English ..."

[13] page 426

Nor need this be seen as a surrender to an oppressive system, as some bitter critics have argued. In making such choices, in the context of the real world in which these people are needed to take a full part in society, there is hope of their obtaining a greater influence on the system itself which they may use constructively.

It is relatively easy to state our two principles. Their practical application in schools and colleges is, however, liable to raise more difficult questions. There is now a substantial body of research literature dealing with the language needs of children from minority groups. It is not our purpose here to catalogue or even to summarise this, but rather to confine our remarks in the rest of this chapter to a number of areas on which we, as practising

26

teachers, feel able to comment from our own experience. We may add, however, in passing that we were surprised by the cursory dismissal of many key issues in *English from 5 to 16 [21]* in the one sentence, "These pupils may need special provision", when the HMI lists of objectives in both spoken and written language skills present difficulties, many of which are certainly rooted in different cultural traditions.

We have been increasingly aware in the last few years of girls and boys from minority groups who may seem to have a few language problems in the early years of schooling but may suddenly experience dismaying failures of understanding in later secondary studies which involve more subtle and metaphorical language. The problem is hard to tackle at this Phase Two stage. It often highlights the fact that allusion, the unifying power in language, is missing, and this may have a cumulatively damaging effect on their understanding. We therefore feel justified in saying it is in their interests that we acquaint these children with enough of the cultural background of English, since the attempt to teach language in an unnaturally restricted form and context does not, in the end, prove sufficiently enabling for them. This point has an important bearing on decisions about the range of reading and literature to which we would introduce them. We must help them to practise the reading between the lines which is so important as well as responses to surface meaning.

These last remarks do not conflict with our other recommendations about sensitivity to and interest in art and culture other than English; nor does our recommendation here conflict with the FEU findings *[23]* that the pupils from such groups who are shrewder in foreseeing the demands of our society seek academic qualifications, not skilled training nor the pursuit of their personal interests – nor leisure courses before the most pressing requirements are secure. Literature can powerfully influence personal and social attitudes as it contributes to the maturing process. It has a significant place in that programme of general language awareness for all pupils which Swann sees as a major part of "education for all" *[13]*.

We take note therefore of the renewal of interest in Bullock's

[25] plea for language concern across the school curriculum as the means of enhancing each individual's chances of "a language for life". We see in the General Criteria for GCSE *[36]* the constant reminders to teachers of all subjects about the importance of spoken and written language, the demand for vigilance in eliminating bias in syllabuses and assessment materials. We agree with Swann that many of the issues to do with the language-learning of students belonging to cultural minorities should be considered as part of the wider context. What exactly are these children's needs and how may we best provide for them?

English as a second language

For children who arrive in this country as first-generation immigrants having little or no English or preparation to cope with massive culture shock and rapid adjustment to an alien, complicated and bewildering society, there is urgent practical need to learn English for immediate reasons of social survival. In many cases this pressure is all the more intense as the child could be the only member of the family receiving any formal education and she or he may thus become the linguistic intermediary between the family and the outside world.

Children from communities which have been established in the United Kingdom for some years but which maintain a clear linguistic separateness from the host community have ESL needs which may seem less urgent but which are, in fact, no less real.

To help children in the first group some local authorities, but by no means all, established and still maintain reception centres. The objectives of such centres are limited as is, frequently, the length of time for which children attend them. Often they have provided little more than a crash course in functional, social, phrase-book English, with some introduction to the more obvious and superficial customs of their host country. After this primitive Berlitz-style programme of cultural immersion, sometimes lasting no more than six weeks or so, the children have been phased into local schools where it is assumed, sometimes fallaciously, that they will make a rapid cultural adaptation from what they learn in the playground as much as in the classroom. In the ordinary school the further language needs of these children are often wrongly assumed to be similar to those of slow learners among the host population: this results often in their being automatically placed in remedial classes. In the majority of cases, we know, this could be a mistake.

The provision of reception centres was always patchy. Some disappeared as a result of the local authorities having to find more and more savings within their education budgets. Four years ago we recommended that local authorities should establish at least one such centre with expert language teachers and the resources to provide systematic tuition in small groups. We also thought then that there should be no arbitrary time-limit within which such help automatically comes to an end for the individual child, whatever the rate of progress. We had wished to see flexibility to make it possible for children to be introduced gradually to the normal school environment over a period, joining their classes full-time when they were linguistically equipped to build on the language foundations so crucial to their learning.

However, Chapter 5 of the Swann Report *[13]* presents a powerfully coherent case for adopting a very different policy. The logic of the arguments expounded there in theory would make us incline to the belief that provision for such pupils should be much more closely linked from the outset with the ordinary school which the children may attend alongside others with whom they should be encouraged to work and play as quickly as possible.

This recommendation by Swann, which appeals strongly to our judgement as teachers, could, unfortunately, be responsibly supported only if we were sure that the ideal conditions for mainstream and minority groups' English language learning were developing rapidly in the vast majority of maintained schools in this country. The ultimate ideal, in our view, would be the enlightened approaches and supportive environment created by a whole staff of teachers with sufficient specialist knowledge and skills. But it is difficult, when the present situation in schools is so unsatisfactory, to feel confident that this change in direction could be easily managed without risk. As Swann rightly says about superficial attempts at integration:

"It would hardly be in the interests of second language learners to lose the specialist help of E2L teachers and be simply left to 'sink or swim' within the mainstream classroom situation without the necessary help and support."

[13] page 395

Whether or not separate units or special help within ordinary schools is the policy, far more resources should be devoted to those needs over a longer period than is often the case. Recent reports have indicated to us that, if children are taught initially in separate units or withdrawn for special help, liaison between teachers and schools in many cases needs to be far better than at present to ensure fruitful co-operation.

We still maintain that money, staffing and equipment are required to provide systematic tuition individually and in small groups while these pupils are sharing as far as possible at the same time in the learning experiences of their contemporaries. We emphasise once again: help is needed well beyond the initial stages.

To equip each school as Swann recommends *([13] §2.10, page 392)* with a well-trained staff for these purposes requires an expensive in-service training programme. Yet we believe such investment is directly in the interests of the wider community because of the far-reaching effects of attitudes inherent in language use – and language awareness.

LEAs should develop such a programme as their longer-term goal for the benefit of both English-speaking and ESL pupils. In the short term LEAs must develop one or more schools with a concentrated group of specialist teachers and extra resources to become the centres of expertise. They can provide extra advisory help in ESL teaching to the surrounding schools, undertaking fuller diagnostic and screening tasks and monitoring progress. This should not ever eliminate the need for

(a) an ESL expert in all schools where there are children whose mother-tongue is not English,

(b) an element in all initial teacher-education which, in our opinion, is essential: that is, a thorough introduction to a language for life *[25]* and the concept of language across the

the curriculum; this must include an insight into some of the basic points of ESL teaching.

We see that extra, properly trained staff may well be needed for the English department of secondary schools if at present several non-specialists, who may not have had the chance to learn about the nature of language skills, help with English teaching. But, beyond that, we strongly endorse the statement in the Swann Report ([13] §§2.12 and 2.14, pages 393–394) that all other teachers with a substantial number of pupils for whom English is a second language should be given appropriate support and training to discharge their responsibility for the linguistic needs of pupils in their own subject areas. We note that the then Secretary of State, in a speech in 1985, admitted the need to give primary children whose first language was not English a sufficient command of language to develop their talents fully. He saw this as "a particular aspect of doing right by every child". He declared that

"… professional experience shows all the language needs of these children are best met within the normal classroom alongside their peers where they can have access from the beginning to all areas of the curriculum".

[26]

He went on to explain that the specialist language teaching-staff which might be required to work alongside class teachers in support of this provision would normally be eligible for Section 11 grant from the Home Office. He also acknowledged that teachers holding posts of special responsibility for language development needed freeing to carry out that role.

We cannot help feeling that, although those remarks show proper concern, the investment and long-term training needed to realise the Swann ideal will probably be greater than the Secretary of State envisaged. We believe that, in practical terms, it will be important to make sure that the present and next few generations of pupils do not suffer by being caught in a transition period between the two policies for provision. The experience of these young people at school or college or elsewhere will determine their attitude in their community in times of stress.

We note with interest that in recent experiments, where

genuinely expert help can be concentrated in a class alongside the normal teaching going on there, the children in the minority group are not the only ones to benefit; the majority group may well gain from the demonstration of this language-learning in the main classroom environment. This links with the experiments in bilingual teaching to which we refer below. We also know from the work of Barnes and others how big an influence the teacher's own use of language can be, but no teacher should be expected to cope alone in a large class, where all pupils may have language difficulties. We also wish to alert authorities and schools to the need for sensible planning to deal with practical details of classroom management and organisation when the main class or subject teacher may not only be joined by an expert ESL teacher but also one or more assistants to help pupils with special educational needs. The situation calls for flexibility and compromise, as well as genuine co-operation.

Mother-tongue teaching

As we have already seen, opinions differ widely about which are the best approaches to encourage a rapid, confident growth in language skills and thereby facilitate other learning. One of the fiercest controversies rages over the use of mother tongue teaching, whether that phrase be taken to mean the teaching of the mother tongue as a study in its own right or the teaching or other subjects through the medium of the mother tongue.

In some European countries there is a policy that all children should have access to education in the medium of their mother tongue throughout their school education. The assumption in these countries has been that families whose first language is not that of the country are likely to remain highly mobile, returning eventually to their original home countries. In this country the expectation is different. The vast majority of people in our minority groups have the intention of staying here permanently. Therefore we have not employed the policy described above. Questions of mother-tongue teaching have remained controversial even in Wales where Welsh is the native language.

We have already stated the principle of respect for the pupil's home language. We should also ask teachers to remember the existing knowledge and ability of the children which could so easily go unrecognised – unused and unsampled for assessment. Their potential bi- or multilingualism must be seen in a positive light and a major shift in teacher opinion is necessary to move the emphasis in this direction. A proper concern to help these children acquire the necessary skills in English must not be allowed to mask, as it so often does, an equally proper pride in multilingualism.

It has been claimed from research evidence that helping children to secure their grasp of language skills in their mother tongue has a beneficial effect on the facility with which they learn English. Swann dismissed this as not substantiated. However, there have been interesting experiments which have gone further than offering such mother-tongue maintenance to the extent of bilingual teaching of culturally mixed classes. Those that have come to our attention have two characteristics in common: they have been in the primary phase and they have been in bi-cultural rather than multi-cultural schools. We have reservations about whether these techniques could usefully operate with more than one large linguistic minority at a time.

Teaching other lessons through the medium of the mother tongue has been a technique seen as a useful short-term strategy either for newly arrived first generation immigrants or for very young children who do not speak English at home. The advantages claimed for this technique were that it kept up the pace of the child's development but could also provide cushioning against the shock of immediate and total exposure to a strange, complex and incomprehensible language. It has indeed been thought necessary not only to cushion children against that shock but to take account of the adults, particularly women and elderly relations within their families, who may speak little or no English and never acquire more. They are insulated and isolated from our society by their inability to communicate even transactionally in the language of the host community. Language teaching for the child without some sort of linked provision for the related adults may create severe learning difficulties and impede the child's progress. We have been very impressed by the work done by some home/school liaison teachers to ease the difficulties at the point of starting school.

We have concluded, however, that we could not support the concept of exclusive mother tongue teaching throughout a child's school life. As Swann points out (*[13]* §*3.15, page 406*), this separates a child from the shared learning of a group and the perceived emphasis is far more on the child's separateness, concentrating on differences, rather than the technique being seen as an unobtrusive aid to an individual. If our schools and colleges do not set out to prepare their pupils for adult life in a society in which the *lingua franca* is English, and is likely to remain so, then the schools are failing these young people. Mother-tongue maintenance is certainly valuable and should be made available whenever possible, but main-course learning in the mother tongue as a long-term strategy would only encourage linguistic escapism from the needs and demands of adult life.

We have listened carefully to powerful evidence from both points of view in the controversy, with members of cultural minorities among the advocates on both sides. In the end we have been most influenced by our concern (shared by many Asian and Afro-Caribbean parents and teachers) that children must not be condemned to linguistic isolation but in language, as in other aspects of culture, they should have the knowledge and skills to enjoy their choice of cultural identification and medium as we described in Chapter 1.

We do not deny that the maintenance of their mother tongue can be a noticeable help to many children, both in terms of exhibiting respect for their own language and in the consequent benefit to their learning of English and other subjects. We would wish this opportunity to be extended beyond the present level with an improvement in the quality of teaching where necessary just as the teaching of language understanding must be further improved in English teaching.

We believe that there are advantages in helping all pupils to acquire a level of literacy in their mother tongue as well as in English. It would be wrong, however, for teachers to make too easy assumptions about which language is the most appropriate one for this purpose for the individual. The question is complicated by the fact that some minority communities use one language as the spoken medium and a different one for written communication. The combination of Punjabi and Urdu in this way is a good example. In such matters schools need to be sensitive to the community's own perception of the need.

In particular, we feel that all our pupils should have the option of studying their home language to public examination level if they so wish. Where a particular language is heavily represented we should like this provision to be made as part of the main school curriculum, alongside other modern languages, and for members of the host community to share the opportunity of learning the language of their near neighbours which may well prove of use in the careers they themselves are choosing to follow. When the provision is contemplated we hope that those responsible will be fully aware of the need to provide courses or develop new courses which really are suitable to meet the differing needs of those pupils studying their own first language and those studying it as a foreign language.

In areas of wide linguistic diversity, however, this will not be possible for more than one or perhaps two at best of the languages most widely represented. The needs of speakers of the other languages will have to be met in other ways. Many of the minority communities are keen to offer such facilities within their own community organisations, and LEAs' support for such initiatives, in terms of both finance and use of premises, has proved a valuable means of encouraging such developments; it ought therefore, in our view, to be more widespread. The point made in the Swann Report is naturally of far-reaching importance in this context as well as in that of the mainstream school: ethnic minority language teachers must be well qualified and seen to be effective in their work if their status and the respect given to their subject and community are to be enhanced. Better training must be possible for them too.

We hear that some schools have introduced "linguistic awareness" courses aimed at giving all pupils experience of a range of languages including some minority-community languages as well as those traditionally taught in English schools. While we see some theoretical advantages of this approach, we are not aware of how well it works in practice.

Dialect speakers

We now turn once again to consider particularly those children in our schools and colleges who use an English dialect with its own syntactical structures and usages which, because it is close to Standard English, is believed by some commentators to cause what they would call dialect interference. Some speakers do have difficulty in mastering the majority's version of "correct" English because they use a version of the language which has developed a highly distinctive character. We are well aware of the heated controversy over definitions in the current debate, yet we do not think the energy required to deal with children's needs should be lost in argument about terms such as "Creole" as long as our two principles are kept in mind.

Many aspects of this situation are parallel for some members of some of the ethnic groups and for certain sections of the host population. There are, in certain geographical areas of the United Kingdom, frequently but not exclusively in lower socio-economic groups, old-established communities whose use of dialect is an important and intimate indication of identity, linking the speaker or writer with his roots; it involves a complex loyalty which must not be threatened while other modes of expression are made possible and available to each individual – alongside the original – for appropriate use at the individual's choice as experience and circumstances widen.

We have noted the phenomenon frequently recorded of children deliberately adopting a much more pronounced form of dialect in mid-adolescence to assert their allegiance to a group, their defiance of the majority and desire to exclude those who do not belong with them. Unless teachers and schools have thought out their own attitudes to different language uses very clearly beforehand, and presented these attitudes so that they indicate unequivocally their interest in and justice towards aspects of different cultures, such behaviour will be particularly hard to judge and to deal with. In turn the teachers must also inform magistrates, employers and other members of the public of the clear policies they are adopting in this matter and the philosophical bases on which they rest.

On the one hand we are totally opposed to any programme aimed at a kind of linguistic genocide or any educational approach which underestimates children's linguistic versatility and seeks to restrict their styles of communication rather than to increase them. We assert our belief that children should be allowed, without either overt or indirect censure, to speak in their mother-tongue dialect and to use it in writing where appropriate situations arise – in stories and accounts of personal experience, for example. Dialect should be accepted as a valid language mode, a part of the spectrum of use available for conscious selection to be made.

We are interested therefore, and in sympathy with, Professor Harold Rosen's recent statement [27], in the context of GCSE English oral assessment, that children should be allowed to use the language which they are most comfortable with. On the other hand, we are wary of any kind of inverted snobbery which, in over-emphasised acceptance and reinforcement of non-standard linguistic forms, is both patronising and limiting.

The fundamental task of the teacher is to increase the linguistic repertoire of all pupils and, whether they belong to linguistic minorities or not, lead them to awareness of the various registers of language, each appropriate and valid in the context in which it is used. The fulfilment of that task is of particular importance to dialect speakers since, in the field of employment, we have reason to suspect that the demand for a "good command of English" often masks a conscious or unconscious unwillingness for quite other reasons to appoint young black people.

It is not because we consider facility in spoken and written Standard English to be a culturally superior norm that we feel special efforts should be made to ensure that the children of minority groups acquire it. Rather it is because failure to do so may too easily be used as an excuse to deny them opportunities which ought to be available to them. Teachers are, in fact, abdicating their responsibilities if they do not intervene in this way but some are still very unsure of their role. What is more, because language is a constantly evolving organism we have to recognise the historical fact of Standard English as a phenomenon and the validity of its currency throughout the world.

To keep the maximum number of opportunities open for pupils without calling into question the validity of the dialectal variants requires great sensitivity on the part of teachers and well-founded professional confidence. Sensitivity comes not merely from goodwill but from knowledge: hence our emphasis on adequate training for English teachers, ESL teachers and teachers of other subjects. We shall develop these points in Chapter 7.

The staffs of schools whose population contains speakers of West Indian varieties of English must contain language specialists with very specific knowledge of this field. Their brief must contain responsibility for devising programmes and obtaining or generating resource materials which will meet the special challenges their pupils meet. To the extent that, as Swann noted, the recommendations of the Bullock Report [25] have not been implemented to the benefit of all our children and young people, the task of those teaching multi-cultural groups is so much harder.

Resourcing and provision

To meet the many challenges posed by the linguistic needs of minority groups may be difficult and expensive of time, effort and resources but we believe the necessity for it to be paramount. Although we have already stated our general opposition to special curricular provision as a blanket treatment for minority groups, we exclude from this the provision of specific language help tailored to individual need. In this case we regard sophisticated provision as essential for any child. If it is not forthcoming then the lack of it will disadvantage these children in turn for the whole of their lives with increasingly tragic consequences in terms of continuing deprivation in social as well as linguistic experience.

For the most part, although there are research projects, multi-cultural and language centres, special units, resource banks and other strategic agencies undertaking valuable work, current provision is still worryingly fragmented so that, too often, individual teachers feel that they have no clear point of reference for obtaining skilled and experienced help or guidance. We therefore recommend the swift establishment of properly funded national co-ordination to ensure that research is more cohesive, to provide a focal point for the referral of local problems and to guarantee that good practice in LEAs and institutions is systematically disseminated. The proposal, some time ago, for a National Centre for Language in Education was one possible means to that end. Similarly, the Select Committee on Home Affairs recommended that:

"the DES should set up a unit concerned exclusively with multi-racial education."

[10]

The Secondary Examinations Council and the School Curriculum Development Committee must seize opportunities not only to address themselves to these questions as frequently as possible, but also to co-ordinate their work and to establish the right priorities between themselves.

Some local education authorities have produced valuable resource material for children from linguistic minorities. We welcome particularly the initiatives taken by ILEA over the provision of books in various mother tongues. Publishers are now showing much more awareness of the need for this kind of material but we should like to see even greater liaison between the teachers and publishers to determine the best way of satisfying needs so that superficial considerations do not prejudice the quality. The Educational Publishers' Council and the National Book League, with their existing links, are able to facilitate structural discussions on the availability of materials which should give the linguistic minorities the help they require.

However, just as the debate over policies has become more sophisticated in the last few years, so in the appraisal of materials we must use more sophisticated criteria as our awareness grows. The impact of language and the recognition of bias need balanced, well-informed and wise handling by advisers and teachers. Help is available in publications by Gillian Klein ([28], [29]) and others.

Public libraries have an important part to play in extending and amplifying the work of schools and colleges through their provision of adult reading. In addition to the books, the inclusion in their reference and lending stock of records and sound and video tapes chosen to make a special contribution to the understanding of our multi-cultural society is essential and it needs to be kept under constant review. The attitudes towards such material are clearly demonstrated in the manner in which these parts of the stock are arranged and displayed. We should like to see teachers more fully involved in consultation with local education and library committees on this matter as well as with individual librarians. The membership of schools in the School Library Association is integral part or a wider picture of local life and provision. This encompasses material in ethnic-minority languages as well as English.

Although some of the materials both in schools and in local libraries are chosen to serve the needs of those in the early stages of learning English, there must be adequate material to cater for continuing language and literary development beyond this level.

Schools' broadcasts have made a very considerable and significant contribution to language work in schools and colleges. The makers have an admirable tradition of sensitive response to changing needs. We hope to see the Schools Broadcasting Council continuing the development of a coherent strategy reflecting the language needs of minority groups of young people.

Above all, whatever specific provision is made, in the form of either courses or resources, it will never be effective unless it is supported in the everyday teaching of all teachers. In this there are obvious implications for every discussion of the curriculum, of the language of assessment (internal and external), and of teacher education whether initial or in-service. These will be examined in detail in Chapters 4 and 5.

Summary of recommendations
3.1   We stand firmly on two principles: the need for an effective command of English and the need to respect and value the pupil's home languge.
3.2   We support a repertoire approach to language.

3.3 Reception centres for newly arrived first-generation immigrants having little or no English are only a minimum starting point. Schemes of provision have not fully developed to ensure special trained help for such pupils within the context of the main classroom activities where we believe their experience must start and continue for the greater part of their life in school.

3.4 We endorse the view upheld by the Swann Report that children from minority groups should share the activities of their contemporaries as early as possible in all aspects of the school's life and curriculum. ESL help should be available for them within this context and there should be no arbitrary time limit at which ESL support is withdrawn.

3.5 Each LEA should develop one or more schools to become centres of expertise in the provision of initial language help for non-English-speaking children. Where the number of such pupils is large we should like to see such centres in most, if not all, schools.

3.6 A major shift in teacher opinion is necessary to ensure that the actual or potential bilingualism of many minority group children is seen in a positive light.

3.7 If the teaching of other lessons through the medium of the mother tongue is tried as a short-term strategy, either for newly arrived first-generation immigrants or for very young children who do not speak English at home, we do not wish to see this involve the separation of the child from his or her contemporaries. We prefer the emphasis to be placed immediately on the sharing of main subject teaching or class activities in English.

3.8 Mother-tongue maintenance is extremely valuable and should be made available wherever possible. In particular all pupils should have the option of studying their mother tongue to examination level.

3.9 Dialect should be accepted as a valid language mode, a part of the spectrum of usage available for conscious selection.

3.10 Language specialists on the staff of any school with a

Creole-speaking population should have within their brief the responsibility for devising programmes and obtaining or generating resource material to meet the special challenges which they and their pupils together must meet.

3.11 Sophisticated provision of specific help tailored to individual need is essential.

3.12 We recommend the swift establishment of properly funded national co-ordination to ensure that research is more cohesive, to provide a focal point for the referral of local problems and to guarantee that good practice is systematically disseminated.

3.13 Public libraries have a role to play in extending and amplifying the language work of the schools.

3.14 Whatever specific language provision is made needs to be supported in the everyday teaching of all teachers.

Points for discussion

- How can teachers convey the value of a repertoire approach to language to those parents who do not appreciate it?:
- How can mother tongue maintenance be made a reality for minority groups with very small numbers in a particular area?
- How can teachers co-ordinate the practical arrangements within the classroom for the successful implementation of support teaching?
- How can a language policy for a school be made a reality?

Chapter 4

The curriculum

The multi-cultural, anti-racist curriculum

The curriculum of a school ought to reflect the society which the school serves, and it should also prepare its pupils for the society which they will enter when they leave school to live in other parts of Britain or overseas where they will be studying and working alongside people from many different cultures. It is difficult to find an unambiguous term for such an education. The Swann Report says:

"The term 'multi-cultural education', appears to have encouraged schools and LEAs in 'all white' areas to believe that the issues involved are of no concern to them since they see themselves as mono-cultural, and the term seems to have been added to the confusion which already exists about the aims and objectives involved. The simple phrase 'Education for all' describes more accurately the desired approach." *[13] page 317*

We have also noted a belief in some quarters that multi-cultural education often fails to deal adequately with the serious problems of racism. To express our convictions we must describe the sort of education we commend as a multi-cultural and anti-racist curriculum for all.

A good definition of the curriculum aims for a multi-cultural society is found in the evidence submitted by the former Schools' Council to the Swann Committee:

"If the education service is to contribute to a harmonious culturally plural society, the curriculum must reflect this objective. It would be possible to say such a curriculum existed when:

1. It was accepted by all sections of society that it was proper and unremarkable to draw on a diversity of cultural sources, and to incorporate a world perspective.

2. Pupils in class or leisure activities feel secure enough to share their own cultural experience with the teachers and their peers."

[30]

In all our schools children from all ethnic groups, not least the children in the host community, need to be made aware of the different cultures that exist within our society, and should be led to some understanding of them. They need to be taught their main characteristics and to be informed of their important customs. They also need to develop an informed respect for those with cultures different from their own. We believe that a school curriculum which uses among its resources material from a wide variety of cultures, showing equal respect for them all, is one of the most important ways of preventing racism and, where it has arisen, helping to eliminate it.

The Rampton Report says:

"A 'good' education should enable a child to understand its own society and to know enough about other societies to enhance that understanding. A 'good' understanding cannot be based on one culture only, and in Britain, where ethnic minorities form a permanent and integral part of the population, we do not believe that education should seek to iron out the differences between cultures, or attempt to draw everyone into the dominant culture. On the contrary, it will draw upon the experience of the many cultures that make up our society and thus broaden the cultural horizons of every child. That is what we mean by 'multi-cultural' education…

"We believe that a curriculum which takes account of the multiracial nature of society is needed for *all* schools, not just those in which there are ethnic minority pupils. There is much truth iin the argument that ignorance and myth about minority groups exist in inverse proportion to their actual presence."

[9] pages 26–27

The Swann Report avoids the term "multi-cultural education" in its recommendation:

"Multicultural understanding has to permeate all aspects of a school's work; and is not a separate topic that can be welded onto existing practices."

[13] page 364

We emphasise this last point. Those aspects of the curriculum which seek to broaden the cultural horizons of all pupils should not be restricted to one special section, shut off from the rest. An awareness of the multi-cultural society in which we live and the place of that society in the world community is so essential a dimension to learning that it should permeate the whole curriculum. There is a need for a refocusing of the overall curriculum and all subject syllabuses in all schools, and not just those with existing multi-cultural populations. When children leave school to enter employment or further and higher education, or even before then if they move from one part of the country to another, at some time nearly all will find themselves living, working and mixing with people from a wide variety of cultural backgrounds. Every child needs to be prepared for this. Where a neighbourhood lacks the cultural diversity which is so significant nationally, schools must make good the deficiencies in order to prepare their pupils for the world which they will enter as adults. While there is much that can and should be done through the curriculum content and materials used, we believe that in such circumstances they need to be supplemented by actual contacts with ethnic minority people: individuals and groups. Visiting speakers can be arranged and even the most mono-cultural areas are not too far from areas with more mixed populations tc allow at least some sorts of the school visits we mention later.

We believe that a curriculum which reaches out to embrace cultural diversity, and which views life from a world, rather than a merely local, perspective, can be as academically rigorous and challenging as one that does not seek to do so. Four areas in which this may be achieved are:

✳ Topics which offer opportunities to consider historical developments in a variety of cultures.

✳ Topics which may be illustrated by reference to contemporary practice in other societies.

✳ Teachers drawing upon the experiences of pupils from the different groups within the school.

✳ Topics which need to be included to counter racism and popular mythologies and misconceptions that support it.

In learning about the various cultural backgrounds from which come the strands of our modern society, there is no greater

45

stimulus than the chance to do so in a class which itself reflects those backgrounds. To miss this opportunity by the sort of programme of black studies, specifically targeted on black pupils, which has been attempted in some places is a bad mistake. We shall return to this point later.

At the same time we acknowledge that minority groups will understandably wish their children to be educated about their own culture, its origins, history, customs, vicissitudes and achievements, in rather more detail than is appropriate for people from different backgrounds. We therefore consider that, wherever possible, school premises should be more widely available to them so that they may complement the school curriculum, as we shall suggest in Chapter 6. We should not wish, however, to see attendance at any resulting courses or activities either made compulsory or automatically restricted to members of the group in question.

The multi-cultural, anti-racist curriculum must apply to all pupils. Just as European pupils must learn to respect Asian, Afro-Caribbean and other communities and cultures, so must the members of these communities learn to respect and understand European and other communities and cultures. When the curriculum of the school positively incorporates material from as wide a variety of cultures as possible every pupil, including those from the majority ethnic group, which is not always European, will see their own represented as one among a spectrum of cultures and not a deviation from a standard national pattern.

The reality in many schools differs quite widely from the targets we have described above. For historical reasons the traditional school syllabus tends to look at the world from a very European, at times almost exclusively a British (not to say English) point of view. Other countries and other cultures are too often depicted, whether historically or geographically, solely through their dealings with Europe. Whole continents with well developed cultures have those parts of their history ignored which pre-date their discovery by European explorers. In particular it is too common for people with non-white skins to be depicted at best as pitiable, at worst as savage. The extreme forms of this traditional approach are, we are glad to note, less common than they were but their influence remains. More subtle dangers lie in syllabuses which deal with aspects of society in which it is possible to make the mistake of taking European social patterns as all-pervading norms. Family life is an example of an area on which discussion is very prone to such errors. Such attitudes not only form barriers to learning for pupils whose ancestral cultures are thus ignored or misrepresented; they are also serious distortions of fact and hence educationally inadequate for all pupils.

Perhaps the most unfortunate misrepresentation of life in the Third World takes place when its basic traditional technologies are illustrated in circumstances which make them look unworthy and unreliable when in reality they are forms of technology very appropriate to the circumstances in which they were developed, a sound application of science, well tested and tried over centuries and often a wiser use of resources than is the norm in the developed world.

The issues involving language are of central importance and have been looked at in some detail in Chapter 3.

Teaching materials

It is of major importance that educational materials in all subjects should come to reflect society nationally and internationally as it really is. Textbooks, charts, illustrations, posters and artwork should show people of different racial origins working and living together. A crowd scene in which no black man or woman appears is almost invariably incomplete: pictures of British cities which depict white inhabitants solely, with no sign of their Indian, African, Caribbean, Chinese and other neighbours, are seriously misleading representations of British society; illustrations of Paris in French language texts, filmstrips or overhead projector transparencies which similarly ignore coloured inhabitants contain an important omission, significant because it subliminally suggests that Britain's multi-cultural population is unique.

No subject should be excused the need for self-examination in this respect. There is no such thing as a neutral subject. No matter how little a subject refers to culture and society it cannot be taught

47

in a cultural or social vacuum. In chemistry, for example, black children receive an important subliminal message if the illustrations always show test tubes in white hands. We are aware that several working groups within the Secondary Science Curriculum Review have produced teaching and other materials showing a wide range of opportunities within science teaching for multi-cultural and anti-racist education.

If we take a world view of scientific and other research it quickly becomes apparent that the original papers appearing in learned journals are produced by people of all races from universities in every country. It is possible to recognise many Asian and Chinese names while Afro-Caribbean authors often have European names. Attemps should be made to refer to such people whenever possible.

Wherever appropriate, black people should be shown in work-roles, but not just as bus conductors, manual workers or nurses. Black teachers, lawyers, doctors, shopkeepers and bank managers should also be depicted. In making this recommendation we are aware that we are being inconsistent: on the one hand we argue that educational materials should reflect our multi-cultural society as it really is; on the other hand we advocate that black people should be shown in roles which relatively few of them occupy at present. Our answer to this is that there are places in Britain where black people do in fact have such jobs and they serve the entire community, but the number is not as high as it should be so we do not think it either naïve or improper to present our minority group pupils with models on which, if they so choose, they could form their career aspirations; nor do we think it an unacceptable essay in social engineering to lead minority groups towards the view that a person's job or status should reflect his skills, abilities and interests rather than be a function of skin colour. For educational materials to show our society as it is is a desirable but limited objective: to go no further risks reinforcing stereotypes which it should be our aim to question.

The Rampton Report recommended that:

"(i) Teachers should examine critically the text books and teaching materials they use and take account of their appropriateness to today's multi-cultural society.

"(ii) LEAs, through their advisory services, should help teachers to keep under review the text books and teaching materials they use and, as resources allow, provide for the replacement of those which display a negative cultural bias."

[9] page 36

In our response to Rampton, AMMA welcomed these recommendations, and especially their emphasis on the necessary critical review being done by teachers themselves and not by any outside agency. But this, of course, requires the teachers to have the right sort of awareness and sensitivity.

When a school, or a teacher, discovers that some of the resource material in use fails such a scrutiny, it may not be in a position to replace it immediately. Even if a suitable replacement is on the market, the necessary finance may not be to hand. In such a situation something can be done in discussion with pupils by looking explicitly at the shortcomings and revealing them for what they are. This needs sensitive handling and can be at best a stop-gap technique. It would be unwise to impose a total ban on specific books and other resources which do not reflect a multi-cultural society, for this would make it impossible, for example, to use such materials to exemplify an unacceptable cultural bias to stimulate discussion as part of a programme of anti-racist education.

In our experience there is still a shortage of teaching materials with the right sort of cultural diversity. The situation is improving, often as a result of teachers offering suggestions and putting pressure on publishers. Teachers looking for appropriate materials to support a multi-cultural approach have been helped by a Schools Council publication, *resources for multicultural education: an introduction [28]*. The biggest problem is showing teachers of all subjects, especially those subjects which appear to be culturally neutral, that these areas are the most important. If their work is not to hinder a multi-cultural view of the world, they need to become familiar with multi-cultural background information which is incidental to the topic being taught, to supplement the anecdotal material given in asides, as background

49

for work sheets and as the context for questions.

Considerable work is being done. *Curriculum opportunities in a multi-cultural Society [31]* and *Agenda for multi-cultural teaching [32]* give guidance for the entire curriculum including most subject areas. *Science education for a multicultural society [33]* is a publication from the Secondary Science Curriculumn Review. *The seeds of history* is an example of a curriculum development from one school. It shows that:

"Science is a normal part of human activity, undertaken and experienced by humankind, in every continent from the beginning of history."

It adds

"This booklet is not multicultural Science and it is not Anti-Racist or Anti-Sexist Science,"

[34]

but it is an effective contribution to education for multi-cultural society. The publications of the World Studies Teacher Training Centre at the University of York are valuable. *Reading into Racism [29]* gives guidance on choosing bias-free books and other materials. Some LEAs have published handbooks of resources available locally and the Centre for World Development has a catalogue of resources for teaching development issues and Britain's interdependence with the Third World which are also useful. Material and information in these and other specialised publications needs to be more widely disseminated in standard textbooks, educational video films and other standard teaching resources. To illustrate the point that much multi-cultural education is most effective when it is part of the background to the curriculum, there are some people who, not seeing the need for change in all-white classrooms, have failed to notice the sort of changes we commend already appearing in new textbooks, TV programmes and other resources used in schools.

Not all aids to learning consist of classroom materials. Programmes of educational visits play a part, often an important one. We believe that such programmes ought increasingly to include first-hand experience of the cultural habits and achievements of our minority groups; they should therefore

50

include visits to mosques and Hindu and Sikh temples, for example, or to exhibitions and activities arranged by ethnic groups. We suggest that such visits are of even greater value when a school's home town provides none of these things. Many school visits cover considerable distances for some other purpose. Why not this one? Nor should such visits be restricted to non-European cultural contacts; for example, Greek, Serbian, Italian and Polish traditions possess a wealth of music, dance and other activities from which all the world would benefit by access. We welcome the initiative of some schools in arranging visits by parties of pupils to India and elsewhere and we emphasise that such visits should be open to all pupils regardless of ethnic origin.

Wider regional and national publicity is necessary if schools are to plan their programme of visits to take into account the opportunities that exist. Where the classroom itself contains people from a variety of cultures, they themselves can produce valuable input to help broaden their colleagues' understanding. Where the school is mono-cultural, the broadening can come only from the curriculum, supported by the kind of extra-mural experiences we have suggested.

Teachers themselves are a part of the pupils' experience of society, and the sort of cultural broadening that we advocate would be helped by the presence in the teaching profession of more members of minority groups. They could add considerably from their own first-hand knowledge and experience to the cultural breadth on which their school's curriculum could draw, and their influence as role-models for their pupils would be great. We shall return to this theme in Chapter 7.

Primary schools

While much attention in the debate about multi-cultural education has been given to the secondary sector, neither the problems nor the opportunities are unique to that sector. Primary schools are not immune to racist attitudes among pupils. We have been told by experienced primary teachers that they frequently see signs of racism in primary schools.

This is not entirely surprising. Children's earliest years are spent in families which shelter and protect them. As they grow, their natural inquisitive nature needs at times to be limited for their own safety. They are told not to go with strangers and they learn to take a more cautious approach to the unfamiliar (the word is significant) than might perhaps come naturally to them. The necessary caution can too easily turn to a less desirable fear and hostility. Families themselves can do much to set the scene for multi-cultural education by leading children into an ever-widening society and a respect for people different from themselves. To the extent that some families miss this opportunity, the schools have to make good the loss.

Primary schools are well placed to teach by example a respect for all cultures and so help to prevent much of the racism which is manifested in older children. The less formal division of activity into discrete subjects than in secondary schools helps considerably. Stories, pictures and other materials from a wide range of backgrounds can relatively easily be incorporated into many aspects of teaching. There is still a shortage of suitable material and we are a long way from the time when all published material for primary schools incorporates material from a sufficiently wide range of ethnic groups to reflect British society as a whole.

The importance of pre-school provision, and of good home links to enable families to help their children to make a good start at school, will be pointed out in Chapter 6, especially in the context of families where the parents are unfamiliar with the British education system and may not themselves be fluent in English. Questions of language are always of central importance, and never more so than in the early years of schooling. It is here that the question of teaching through the medium of the mother tongue is often raised. In the early school years, when used wisely, as the Schools Council Mother Tongue Project and other research on bilingual teaching has shown, this technique is very useful. It would appear to be particularly commendable when children begin to recognise some words and phrases from each other's languages through printed displays and oral lessons.

Issues of language affect all parts of the curriculum, as is illustrated in this excerpt from the Cockroft Report on Mathematics teaching:

"Especial care is likely to be needed with young children in the early stages of naming numbers and counting. Almost all European languages show irregularities in the naming of some or all of the numbers between 10 and 20. In English, for example, numbers from 13 to 19 are spoken 'back to front' compared with numbers from 20 onwards, so we say twenty-*four* but *four*teen; the words 'eleven' and 'twelve' are even more irregular. In the major Asian languages, each number up to 40 has its own name. Those who teach children whose first language is not English therefore need to take steps to find out about the number system which is used in the countries from which the children's families originate so that they can be aware of the kinds of difficulties which may arise."

[35]

The strong tradition in primary schools for use of lots of display material creates opportunities to express a view of the world in forms with high impact on the sensibilities of the pupils, and everything we have said about teaching materials applies here. The Rampton Report suggests that a good indicator of whether a primary school has responded to the fact of our multi-cultural society is to be found in the representation of members of minority groups in display material around the building. The report quotes with approval one infants' school whose head told them:

"In order to present children of all races with a positive self image, pictures are displayed of people from other cultures in professional occupations. Stories, music, poetry and religious education from other cultures are used constantly. Our latest venture is to photograph the children's parents at their work, in their uniforms, at home and at worship, to provide our own visual aids."

[9] page 31

Secondary schools

One of the features which distinguishes the curriculum of secondary schools from the primary curriculum is the former's greater degree of compartmentalisation into subject areas. The syllabuses of all subjects need to be examined to ensure that they take account of the cultural, social, religious and economic experience and perspectives of all members of our society, not just the native British majority. This contention has clear implications for all subjects. As we have already pointed out, even subjects whose content is in some sense neutral need to take care of their presentation. Where relevant, courses in all subjects should acknowledge the customs and preferences of minority groups; for example, information about Asian and Caribbean foods should be included in the study of cookery and of food tests in science.

We are aware of a number of experiments in which elements of a particular ethnic emphasis – Caribbean studies for instance – have been introduced into the school's curriculum as an option. We think it highly significant that in many cases they have been subsequently withdrawn (and much of the thinking behind them incorporated into the main school curriculum through a number of subjects at different levels in the school) because, taken up almost exclusively by members of the appropriate ethnic group, they have unintentionally reinforced a sense of cultural alienation rather than promoted a feeling of identity. We do not think that it ought to be the function of a school to provide specific ethnically oriented courses for any minority group as an option which prevents those pupils who opt for them from studying other subjects which are more obviously useful as a preparation for employment and further and higher education.

However, we would welcome the provision of courses in the languages of ethnic minority groups within the school provided they are arranged in such a way that pupils from the host community (and other groups) may be included. Indeed we believe that much more esteem should be given to such languages. The multilingual nature of British society today is a resource for strengthing international relations and trade which the nation needs to encourage. A knowledge of one of these languages would be a valuable qualification for both black and white members of many professions, the police and welfare services.

The main objective of our schools and colleges must be to ensure that all pupils, regardless of cultural background, enjoy the same spectrum of options leading to the same range of vocational, academic and professional qualifications. Within that broad aim, pupils should be afforded the chance to pursue courses of study which, tailored to their particular abilities and aptitudes, will fit them for the demands of adult life as full members of society, while respecting the cultural values of their homes and communities.

In Chapter 3 we discussed the question of mother-tongue teaching. In the secondary sector we reject the technique of teaching other subjects through the medium of the mother tongue as inappropriate except in the very special case of newly arrived immigrants with no English. We would like to see, however, all pupils having access to courses in their native language to public examination level, and suggested in that chapter how this might be achieved in areas of wide cultural and linguistic diversity, where the problems are harder than in circumstances where the non-English-speakers are predominantly from a single group. We also said in that chapter that we would encourage pupils from the host community to learn the languages of their neighbours. The Home Affairs Committee recommendations included the following:

"The Department of Education and Science should actively encourage the incorporation of Asian languages into the modern language curriculum. Statistics of examinations taken in these languages should be published annually."

[10]

In fact, most of the mother tongues of those minority groups which are statistically significant nationally were available at GCE O-level at least and we expect them to be more widely available, and more widely taken up, in GCSE with better provision for the levels equivalent to CSE.

We are aware of such courses, often leading to 16+ examinations, successfully being held in community schools and Saturday schools, the examinations being entered through the pupils' own schools and paid for in the same way as the normal school subjects. We note with concern that the General Criteria for

GCSE state that:

"'External candidate' examinations will not be available to candidates in full time attendance at schools and colleges."

[36]

It would be unreasonable for pupils in full-time attendance at a school or college who were able and willing to attend part-time courses in their mother tongues, cultures and religions to be denied certification because the institution was unable to provide tuition and unable to meet the demands for course-work and other requirements set out in the national criteria for such subjects.

Further education

In further education the position is more complicated. For students doing full-time GCSE and GCE A-level courses, particularly in tertiary colleges, the position is similar to that in secondary schools. There are also many part-time students, often studying single subjects. The majority of students are following more advanced academic and vocational courses which appear to be culturally neutral both in their content and in the context in which they are taught. In the same colleges there are often special courses, such as access courses, intended primarily for members of minority groups.

The take-up of courses by students from ethnic minorities needs to be monitored. Explanations need to be sought for differences between the percentage of each minority in the FE college and in the general population of the districts it serves. The overall figures for the college, including those students on courses provided specifically for ethnic minorities, may conceal imbalances in the percentage of students from minority groups on academic and vocational courses. Each course needs to be monitored separately.

Colleges should ensure that each subject is taught within a multi-cultural, anti-racist context. This means, for example, that letters and documents for shorthand, typing and business studies exercises and projects should reflect the composition of British society as a whole. We welcome the work which has been done in some places where engineering projects to design equipment for countries in the third world have been undertaken, especially when this has been based on a thorough study of traditional equipment in those countries and modern technology has been used to complement local skills and resources rather than replacing them with equipment which they would have to import.

Another factor for consideration is the publicity material produced by FE colleges. This needs to be aimed at minority communities as well as society as a whole. Publicity material in Asian and other languages is appropriate for all courses, even those where proficiency in English is essential, because students choices are often influenced by their parents who may not be fluent in English and have little understanding of British vocational qualifications. The lack of take-up by some groups has been shown to be caused by their lack of information about what is available and this could be remedied by directing the normal publicity material to places where social minorities live and work and by advertising in ethnic minority and community publications.

We commend the publication *"Black Perspectives on FE Provision"* particularly as it is based on the views of members of local black communities. It says of its own projects:

"The projects themselves give practical expression to a policy in which future initiatives can be determined *by* rather than *for* the black population."

[37]

The curriculum for vocational courses in further education is largely determined by the needs of employers and professional bodies, while the non-vocational courses are often provided in response to demands from local communities. Minority communities have the same right and need to be consulted.

Progress to date and ways ahead

A good summary of the situation a few years ago came in a 1981 Schools Council pamphlet:

"(i) 'Special' needs

"There is now widespread acceptance in multi-racial areas of the need to make arrangements to meet the 'special' needs of minority ethnic groups; however, in terms of actual provision this still in practice largely means meeting the basic language requirements of English as a Second Language learners ... there has been little generation of resources to identify and meet other special needs.

"(ii) Curriculum in multi-racial schools

"The major change ... is that many of those responsible for and involved in multi-ethnic education within authorities and in schools now believe that the presence of minority ethnic group children has implications that go beyond the need for special arrangements and special provision and involve the curriculum generally. Curriculum development in these schools is now seen less in terms of simply adding on special subjects – such as 'black studies' – and more as involving a reappraisal of the curriculum as a whole to make it relevant (in the context of today's aims and objectives) to all pupils.

"(iii) Curriculum in schools with few or no minority ethnic group pupils

"Within authorities in multi-racial areas there is now wide agreement that the presence of minority ethnic groups in Britain has implications for the curriculum in all schools whatever their ethnic composition, but competing priorities and limited resources mean that little action is currently being taken in schools with few or no minority ethnic group pupils. In authorities where there are few or no such pupils the general view is that the wider multi-ethnic society has little relevance for their schools."

[38]

Six years later we see little change in the situation. Ethnic minorities are less confined to a few areas than was then the case, with the effect that there is a significantly greater number of schools with some children from these groups. In most of these cases, however, the proportion of such children is small and the less aware teachers in the schools have not yet woken up to the need to review their curriculum from a multi-cultural point of view. Since the publication of our previous document *[12]*, members of our working party have often been approached by AMMA members who tell us that they have read the booklet, realise that it has implications for their school but despair of communicating this

this awareness to the bulk of their colleagues.

A number of LEAs have introduced multi-cultural or anti-racist policies, including curriculum policies. Some of these have been well thought out and subject to consultation with teachers have met with some success. Others have been hastily devised without consultation and discussion. The latter group have, on the whole, been counter-productive, producing more irritation than understanding among teachers.

There has been some progress in schools with few ethnic minority pupils. The Swann Report contains, as Annexe D to Chapter 5, a report by Laurie Fallows (a former county adviser in Lancashire) of visits to a number of such schools. Of one infants' school he writes:

"The Head's stated philosophy includes 'Within all our work we try to help children to develop a good self-image, to be considerate and caring in their relationships, to grow in self awareness, to develop an awareness of the needs of others…' These objectives are fully in concord with the principles of multi-cultural education, and it is probably not unfair to say that in part they reflect a response to the needs of minority group children, Travellers and handicapped within the school community, into which the Head and other teachers have been involved in extensive study.

"The curriculum follows traditional lines, but it is noteworthy that in recently changing the reading syllabus, the staff had sought a basic scheme that would help to 'broaden the children's horizons'. They settled for 'Reading 360' (Ginn) that introduced naturally children and adults of other ethnic groups. Some of their back-up readers extend this experience."

[13] pages 277–278

Of a large comprehensive school in a small market town, the same report says:

"In many ways it presents close similarities with other schools in that it perpetuates regional characteristics through an inward-looking, self-conscious and defensive parochialism that is apathetic to conditions and issues beyond its immediate experience and influence. In others it suggests a desire from its more enlightened members to leap beyond its self-imposed boundaries into an emancipated, more tolerant pluralist society."

[13] pages 292–293

Much was done by the Schools Council to raise teachers' awareness of the need for a multi-cultural approach to the curriculum and to develop suitable materials. Some of this work is continuing under the auspices of the School Curriculum Development Committee. The BBC has also made a significant contribution. We commend especially their series of programmes for teachers *Case studies in multi-cultural education* [39] and the accompanying book [40].

But there is still much that needs to be done in raising the awareness of the need for a multi-cultural and anti-racist approach to the curriculum and to disseminate existing good practice. There are many teachers who are coming to an understanding of the needs but who need help and advice about how to respond and how to find the materials for which they begin to see the need.

Summary of recommendations

4.1   In all our schools children from all ethnic groups, not least the children of the host community, need to be made aware of the different cultures that exist within our society, and should be led to some understanding of them.

4.2   There is need for a multi-cultural focus in the curriculum and subject syllabuses in all schools, not just those with existing multi-cultural populations.

4.3   We do not think that it ought to be the function of a school to provide specific ethnically oriented courses for any minority group.

4.4   The main objective of schools must be to ensure that all pupils, regardless of cultural background, enjoy the same curricular opportunities.

4.5   School premises should be more widely available to minority communities so that they may complement the school curriculum to extend their children's knowledge of their own background beyond the level that is appropriate in the main school.

4.6 Textbooks and all teaching and display materials should show people of different racial origins working and living together. Black people should be shown in professional as well as manual work-roles.

4.7 Teachers, helped by the advisory service, should scrutinise their teaching materials to assess their suitability to today's multi-cultural society.

4.8 Good practice needs to be disseminated, and there is still a need to raise the consciousness of those LEAs and teachers who have not yet realised the importance of these issues.

4.9 FE courses, including vocational courses, should be taught in a multi-cultural and anti-racist context.

4.10 The take-up of FE provision by students from ethnic minorities needs to be monitored, course by course, to identify any imbalance and bias.

Points for discussion

* How much study of a particular culture is appropriate within the main school curriculum and how much should be seen as the province of the minority community?
* How can we insert a world perspective into the whole width of the curriculum?
* How can the range of available classroom materials relevant to our multi-cultural society be improved?
* How can we eliminate bias and institutional racism from our teaching and our materials?

Chapter 5

Examinations

The inter-relation between public examinations and the curriculum is complex. The philosophy of the curriculum leading the examinations is a valuable one, but not a good description of the day-to-day reality in schools. In the interplay of cause and effect between the two sides, it more often appears that the examination system is limiting curriculum development, or at best slowing it down, rather than being as responsive to curriculum development as many teachers would like. It certainly cannot be denied that the examination system has been a powerful shaping force on the curriculum. What then should be the aims of public examinations in the context of multi-cultural and anti-racist education?

First of all, the examinations need to reflect the curriculum. Since we have argued that the curriculum should draw on the whole range of cultures that form the background of our mixed society, then it follows that the examinations should do the same, both (where relevant) in the actual subject syllabuses and in the examples taken in the questions. It further follows that we do not think there is need for any widespread introduction of special public examination subjects or syllabuses for ethnic minority pupils (with the exception of examinations in their mother tongues), but rather for a concerted effort by all examination boards to keep their syllabus content and actual examination papers under constant review as we have proposed for the curriculum, to see that both syllabuses and questions reflect the multi-cultural nature of contemporary society. As with the curriculum, we do not believe that this would lead to any lowering of standards.

Some boards make this a responsibility of subject panels. If such a responsibility is to be exercised properly, these panels need access to the appropriate expertise, both among their panel members and from one or more specialist officers of the examination group or board. The Examinations Standing Joint Committees of the teacher unions and associations should add a multi-cultural dimension to the criteria by which they review the work of the examination groups.

In our earlier publication *[12]* we said that there had been a movement in the directions we advocated since the "picture of conservative over-cautiousness" revealed by a Schools Council survey in 1980 *[41]*. This movement has continued.

The Swann Report recommended:

"Examining boards should reflect cultural diversity in the syllabuses they offer and in their working practices.

"The Secondary Examinations Council should cooperate with the School Curriculum Development Committee to ensure that initiatives to broaden the school curriculum are reflected by parallel developments within the examination system."

[13] page 365

The national criteria for the GCSE have responded to this:

"Every possible need must be made to ensure that syllabuses and examinations are free of political, ethnic, gender and other forms of bias.

"In devising syllabuses and setting question papers Examining Groups should bear in mind the linguistic and cultural diversity of society. The value to all candidates of incorporating material which reflects this diversity should be recognised."

[36] General Criteria, §19 (h) & (i)

AMMA has written to the Secondary Examinations Council to ask how these criteria are monitored. We received the following reply:

"I can assure your Multicultural Working Party that our Committees have always taken account of these Criteria and we would claim that the Examining Groups are much more aware of these issues than they used to be. However, as the Working Party will realise, it is one thing to approve the syllabus, it is another thing to make sure the actual examination papers in 1988 also meet those Criteria. It is of course the responsibility of the Examining Groups to see that they do so, but we shall be carrying out scrutinies of the GCSE Examinations and I am sure that these aspects will be looked at as stringently as any."

[42]

Outside the orbit of the GCSE, other examining bodies are also responding to the views of those teachers who are trying to bring a multi-cultural perspective to their teaching and are looking for examinations which will give expression to this. The Joint Board for the CPVE, for example, included a section in the social skills part of its core competences which clearly embraces, among other things, an anti-racist perspective:

"AIM 4: CATEGORIES OF GROUPS

"To recognise and analyse the signs used to allocate individuals to categories, and to be aware of the prevalence and abuses of such categorisation by …

4.2 identifying factors used in placing people into categories – gender, class, race, dress, speech, age …

4.4 recognising misuses of categorisation of individuals and groups – working, social, cultural and religious.

4.5 recognising own and others' reactions to being placed in categories."

[43] page 11

Examinations also need to be culturally fair by elimination of any hidden bias against minority group candidates. The sort of broad cultural base that we have advocated should go part of the way towards that, but cannot be the whole story. Attention also needs to be given to the language in which examination questions are couched and in which the answers are expected. We heard in the past of cases of particular examinations in science subjects penalising candidates for describing experiments in first-person narrative. We have already argued (in Chapter 3) that an ability to communicate in English, including its more formal registers, is a prerequisite for success in many aspects of life. We believe that examinations should properly reflect this but that such requirements can be, and sometimes are, over-formalised to the detriment of some candidates who are highly conversant with the subject matter of the exam but have not yet achieved full mastery of formal English. Pupils for whom English is not their first language, or whose language takes a strong dialect form, will be disproportionately handicapped by inappropriate language requirements.

The GCSE examinations include the assessment of reporting and communications skills among their criteria, not only in English but across the board. For example, the National Criteria for Biology include among their aims:

"To develop a range of manipulative and communicative skills appropriate to the subject"

[36] Biology §2.3.1

and among their assessment objectives:

"Candidates should be able to … select and communicate this information cogently in a variety of ways."

[36] Biology §3.2.7

It is obviously better to make actual specifications rather than to rely on unwritten understandings between examiners and teachers.

The GCSE also provides a bigger place for assessed oral work than in the examinations it supersedes, not only in English and other language examinations but also more generally:

"The scheme of assessment should normally offer an appropriate combination of board-assessed components and centre-assessed course-work."

[36] General Criteria 19(e)(iv)

The course-work component gives the opportunity for assessment of practical work in a whole range of subjects to be based in part on oral answers and discussion. This we feel will help to reduce the effect of any accidental bias in written examinations against candidates whose first language is not English and who may communicate more fluently and clearly in spoken English. Conversely it will no longer be the case that entirely written examinations give an exaggeratedly high score to candidates whose strengths and weakness are the other way round.

The CPVE also stresses aspects other than literacy in the communication section of its core competences, dividing these into listening, speaking, reading, writing, communication and interpretation *([43] pages 8-9)*.

65

We have already mentioned more than once our support for the availability of public examinations in the languages of Britain's minority groups. Until now there has been a low take-up of such examinations. It is regrettable that there have been very few minority community languages available in the CSE and we believe that more development is necessary to ensure that more are available in the GCSE. This will not come on a large scale until there is pressure from teachers and minority communities to bring about changes which will give the same esteem to these languages as to French and German.

One aspect of examinations which cannot be ignored, and which was given an airing in the Rampton Report, is the conviction on the part of many people of West Indian background that British schools have tended to channel children from such a background into CSE rather than O-level courses. Rampton found:

"This concern is borne out to some extent by the results of the school leavers' survey exercise which show that in the six LEAs covered, 46% of West Indian pupils were entered for CSEs only, compared with a national average 33%. Whether this is indeed the result of low teacher expectations or simply a consequence of the overall underachievement of West Indian pupils is clearly something we need to consider further and on which we need further evidence."

[9] page 39

If this is indeed the product of low teacher expectation of this group of pupils, and we believe that this is likely to be true (although the expectation may well be unconscious) in many cases, then there is need for vigilance lest the same syndrome finds expression through the use of the differentiated papers of some subjects in the GCSE. This is potentially more insidiously dangerous since it is less immediately obvious to parents and the community.

Much work has been going on nationally and in many LEAs to develop profiles and records of achievement, both in conjunction with and separate from formal examinations. In the post-16 age range, and hence in the FE sector, it currently has a much wider occurrence than in 11-16 work in schools. Discussion of this development has identified few direct implications concerned with the multi-cultural society.

Language, as always, is of central importance and we would urge that people devising such schemes should pay heed to the ideas of our Chapter 3 and Swann's Chapter 5. Criterion-referenced profiles may provide a fair way of describing the language achievements of pupils from non-English-speaking backgrounds, but we continue to have reservations about some schemes which require all teachers, not just language specialists, to make sophisticated assessments of pupils' command of English. To do so fairly, in the context of our Chapter 3, would require a greater level of expertise about language than many non-specialist teachers have at present. The successful introduction of schemes with such a feature will therefore depend particularly heavily on the availability of suitable INSET provision for all teachers.

Academic profiling can potentially respond more rapidly to curriculum development than can formal examinations and hence can give earlier expression to improvements along the lines of our Chapter 4.

Summary of recommendations

5.1   Examinations should draw on the whole range of cultures in our society, both (where relevant) in their subject syllabuses and in the examples taken in the questions.

5.2   Examinations should not contain any hidden bias against minority group candidates. Attention needs to be given to the language in which examinations questions are couched and in which the answers are expected.

5.3   Examination subject panels need access to the appropriate expertise to enable them to review their syllabuses and papers from a multi-cultural and anti-racist perspective.

5.4   The Examinations Standing Joint Committees of the teacher unions and associations should add a multi-cultural dimension to the criteria by which they review the work of the examination groups.

5.5   There is need for vigilance to see that differentiated papers in the GCSE are not used in ways that discriminate against minority groups.

5.6   Academic profiling needs to give an important place to questions of language, but we have reservations about schemes which require teachers other than language specialists to make sophisticated judgements in this area. Such schemes have major INSET requirements.

Points for discussion

✳ How can the suitability and availability of examinations in the mother tongues of minority groups be improved?

✳ How can examination papers in the whole range of subjects be made to reflect the multi-cultural society?

✳ To what extent should examiners in non-linguistic subjects expect candidates' answers to be expressed in a particular register of language?

✳ How can teachers ensure that oral assessments do justice to pupils with non-standard language backgrounds?

Chapter 6

School and beyond

School and community

The Swann Report said:

"We believe that a genuinely pluralist society cannot be achieved without the social integration of ethnic minority communities and the ethnic majority community within a common whole. Whilst we are *not* looking for the assimilation of the minority communities within an unchanged dominant way of life, we are perhaps looking for the 'assimilation' of *all* groups within a redefined concept of what it means to live in British society today. We are not seeking to fit ethnic minorities into a mould which was originally cast for a society relatively homogeneous in languages, religion and culture, nor to break this mould and replace it with one which is in all senses 'foreign' to our established way of life. We are instead looking to recast the mould into a form which retains the fundamental principles of the original but within a broader pluralist conspectus – diversity within unity."

[13] page 8

If the recommendations of the report are to be successfully implemented in schools, the first essential is a deep level of mutual understanding between the school, the home and the wider community, specifically including ethnic minority groups within that community.

Within each ethnic minority group there are individuals with very different views about the extent to which they would seek to assimilate with the host community. Some will aspire to complete social, linguistic and cultural integration. Others will wish to preserve their distinct cultural identity by maintaining a clear separation from the majority group in matters of language, religion, diet and social customs. Yet others will seek a middle way, retaining elements of their own cultural identity in a context of the wider pluralist environment. Such people will find ways of adjusting their own traditions to the world of school, work and the daily transactions of life.

We affirm that it is the right of individuals to make this choice for themselves. It is part of the task of schools whose intake contains pupils from ethnic minorities to educate all of them for such a choice. This involves giving the pupils the necessary information and skills they will need if the choice is to genuinely available to them and is to be an informed one. To do this without seeming to attack attitudes, possibly quite different, within pupils' families requires that deep understanding between the school and its community to which we have already alluded.

For some minority groups, the parents' experience of education in other parts of the world leads to misunderstanding about the British education system. In some cases this takes the form of an excessive reverence for teacher and a reluctance to interfere in school matters. Such parents are unlikely to take the initiative in coming into the school or to respond easily to invitations to do so. It is for the school to go out and make contact with them.

For others again, as Swann pointed out, there is the fear of attack on the way to school.

Cultural differences may make for practical difficulties. Too often because the school and the home have different ways of expressing their care for a child, neither side can recognise the other's actions for what they are – expressions of care. So the parents end up suspicious of the school and the school feels that the parents are not supportive.

There is a great need for a mutual reaching-out to build up understanding. Conventional Parent-Teacher Associations have too often had very limited success in this respect. Too often the PTA represents a small proportion of the socio-economic and ethnic groups in the community served by the school. In some areas the education welfare service makes a degree of contact, but this is limited and comes into play only when a child is already in trouble. Recent legislation has emphasised the need for closer links between parents and the school. The representation of parents on governing bodies, already happening in many areas,

70

can help. But this also depends on the active participation of parents from across the whole range of groups in the wider community.

We have reservations about the Rampton Report's solution that:

"Schools should encourage teachers to see home visiting as an integral part of their pastoral responsibility."

[9] page 46

While home visiting is vitally important in the context, we doubt whether the teaching profession has yet reached a stage where all teachers (or even all of those with designated pastoral responsibility) are capable of doing it effectively between the home and the host community, especially if there are also differences of languages. In any case if all teachers were to try to visit the homes of even a representative selection of their pupils, the sheer load of visits would become impractical, both for the teacher and for the home, especially in the case of secondary schools.

It should be possible to establish training programmes for teachers to give them a deeper knowledge and understanding of the people with whom they need to establish links on the school's – and the child's – behalf. One requirement is the knowledge of the etiquette and courtesies which each community associates with visits to the home. Initial contact by letter may not always be appropriate: it could be misunderstood or create apprehension.

Social mixing in the minority community by teachers, preferably involving visits to homes (not necessarily of pupils) of different cultural background from their own, could offer valuable and relevant insights. Schemes for encouraging this could possibly be arranged by PTAs, minority group organisations or Community Relations Councils.

Until more teachers have the necessary skills, schools need to identify which members of staff are capable of being most effective at home visiting and then give them the responsibility (and the time) to do it, making sure that the lines of communication within the school are good enough to disseminate to all colleagues the benefit gained from home visits.

71

Some LEAs have already established posts for home-school liaison teachers, based either in a single school or at a centre serving several. They provide an invaluable link between the school's pastoral staff and the pupils' homes. Where minority communities may contain significant numbers of adults with little or no fluency in English, a liaison teacher fluent in one or more of the community languages can make an immense contribution.

Maintaining responsive links between school and home is vitally important but costly in staff time. It must be resourced by modifying the staffing of schools which have significant numbers of minority group pupils so that existing staff have sufficient time: alternatively the kind of liaison teachers we have mentioned need to be appointed.

Attention also needs to be given to the language of written communication with the home, whether originating from the school or the education office. In some areas it is already the practice for such communications to be available in locally significant minority languages and we are pleased to note that this practice appears to be spreading. Even in English attention must be paid to the register of language in such documents so that they can readily be understood by parents who may be less than fluent in the more formal registers.

The sooner the links between home and school are forged the better they will function. The time of entry to school is vitally important. Starting school can often be a difficult experience for both child and parent: how much more so in the context of mutual misunderstanding that we have described in the case of some minority groups. When a home-school liaison teacher from Birmingham came to talk to our working party it was this aspect of her work that she told us most about. We believe this to be a necessary emphasis. The Rampton Report included as an appendix (*[9] pages 88-105*) an example of a leaflet issued by one LEA to parents with young children to help them prepare their children and themselves for the experience of starting school and to inform them of the available health and welfare services. This is an example which we should like to see become common. In some areas such a leaflet would need to be available in a range of languages.

There are many things that minority communities can bring to enrich the life of schools. The very presence in a school of representatives of minority groups (pupils and, it is to be hoped, teachers) is itself a stimulus which can be channelled into a valuable learning experience. This can be extended by reaching out via these individuals to the communities they come from. In the section of Chapter 4 dealing with primary schools we quoted an example in which photographs of parents of the class were used as a learning resource. In another part of the same chapter we advocated educational visits to minority community activities.

Many minority communities have their own educational activities. Some of these are designed to complement the school curriculum by teaching children about their own cultural background, religion and language. The amount of detailed study of any one cultural group that is appropriate within a main school curriculum for all pupils will almost certainly fall short of what that group will feel necessary for its own children. There would be much mutual benefit if schools could link up with such activities at an informal level, if only by lending their buildings for the purpose. Even to do no more than this would demonstrate respect for the acceptance of the minority group's traditions and culture. In fact the experience of bringing minority-group adults into the school building, and the contacts that would result, could have a wide-reaching beneficial effect.

Another kind of minority-group educational activity occurs most often in the West Indian community where many parents, seriously worried about the underachievement of their children in school, have banded together to form supplementary schools to provide tuition in basic skills. The parents concerned show a very high level of commitment to such schools. While we, as teachers in the main school system, may feel regret at the things that make these parents feel the need for supplementary schools, in our pupils' interests we ought to find out what we can about them and co-operate with them.

The biggest resource available from any community is its people, and there is much to be gained by involving more members of minority groups in the process of education as teachers, administrators, welfare and career officers, school and college governors and elected members of LEAs. Recruitment of teachers from minority groups will be considered in Chapter 7. Similar arguments apply to the other professions mentioned. At school level the representation of minority groups on governing bodies (and not only in their role as parents) can bring valuable insights. Since our previous publication we have noted an increase in such representation in some parts of the country, but there is still a long way to go. We look forward to the day when our political system will operate to produce fairer representation of minority groups on elected bodies in local and national government.

After school

As long ago as 1969, Frank Cousins, who was chairman both of the Central Training Council and of the Community Relations Commission, said:

"The future integration of coloured workers depends to a large extent on coloured children gaining apprenticeships and entry into skilled and white collar occupations ... Unless coloured workers are helped and encouraged to obtain training, the accumulation of a residue of untrained, unemployed and unemployable coloured workers is a possibility which cannot be excluded. If we are content to have a group of people untrained and unemployable, they will become unfriendly and the neglected part of society with an additional grievance to bear."

[44]

While we hold no brief for the view of integration implicit in these words, we believe them to have been prophetic. In his report on the 1981 riots in Brixton, Lord Scarman said:

"Unemployment is a problem which faces both white and black people. There is evidence, however ... that its weight falls disproportionately heavily on black people. Unemployment among black people is no doubt mainly the result of factors which also affect the employment prospects of the white community. But there are other factors peculiar to the black community, for as the Home Affairs Committee notes in paragraph 168 of their report *[10]* 'Asians and West Indians continue to be at a substantial disadvantage in employment long after arrival in Britain and their children may also suffer substantial disadvantage in this respect'. The Select Committee note various possible reasons for this, of which racial discrimination, past and present, is one of the more important."

[8]

Five years after Lord Scarman's words and seventeen after Mr Cousins', the problem still faces schools preparing young people for adult life. For many, whether black or white, in their final year at school there must be the strong temptation, even with the presence of YTS, to give in to the "Why bother? What's the use?" syndrome, especially in areas of high unemployment.

There are a number of reasons why young black people find more difficulty than their white contemporaries in looking for work. Direct prejudice on the part of many employers is certainly one. It has long been known that skin colour is the dominant factor in such prejudice. A study in Lewisham, conducted in 1977 and published the following year *[45]*, confirmed this result which had been found in an earlier study in Nottingham. The frequent demand that "applicants should have a good command of English" is often used as a cloak for such prejudice.

For Afro-Caribbean youngsters the problem is exacerbated by their educational underachievement as a group, which was clearly identified in the Rampton Report *[9]*. In *the education of the black child in Britain [46]*, Maureen Stone argues that the failure of our education system to deliver its benefits effectively to working-class children automatically works to the disadvantage of black children, many of whom are in this group.

Minority-group members are much less likely to have the wide range of informal contracts for job-hunting – "Uncle Fred in the print" – that is available to so many of the majority group.

There is evidence that the Afro-Caribbean community tends to mistrust the careers service. The Rampton Report found:

"West Indian parents feel strongly that some careers officers arbitrarily restrict the range of opportunities presented to their children either because of the local situation or because of a lack of sensitivity which can be perceived as discrimination. There is a feeling among West Indian parents that careers officers, like careers teachers, have discriminatory views of young West Indians which lead them to channel them into certain occupations...

"All the careers officers we spoke to when preparing this report referred to a lack of knowledge and understanding on the part of West Indians and their parents of the employment market in this country. The careers officers all said that young West Indians were underachieving but despite this their parents often had unrealistically high career aspirations for them. The youngsters on the other hand were said to have career aspirations within a rather narrow and limited range; as one career officer put it to us; 'they all want to be motor mechanics'."

[9] page 57

It is to be hoped that, to the extent that the phenomena reported by those careers officers were real, they will diminish with passing time as a greater proportion of the parents of West Indian youngsters have themselves been brought up in this country. But we are aware of no evidence to show whether such a change has begun. Schools and the careers service have worked together to try to alleviate these difficulties, but their resources are limited and the commitment has been patchy. Two researchers reported in 1975:

"What became obvious in our study was the extent to which careers guidance is still a matter of individual interest and motivation. While there appeared to be a general recognition that the authorities considered such guidance as a 'good thing' many had not the resources and few had a clearly defined idea of what could be done. This is not surprising, given the undeveloped state of official thinking on the matter and, equally, the inadequate provision of in-service training and other resources necessary to do the job."

[47]

There is a demonstrable short-fall here between the will, on the part of central and local Government, that something should be done and their willingness to provide the means for doing it.

But this is not the whole story. We are aware of some schools where young people are leaving school without having been taught the techniques of writing a letter of application, although we are at a loss to see how this can come about. Even if a school offers no class careers lessons and no life skills programme, we would hope that the repertoire approach to English teaching which we advocate and which is becoming more dominant would have covered this particular mode of writing.

We believe that, given the resources, our schools can do more to prepare our pupils, minority and majority alike, for adult life. This involves much more than equipping them to find a job – although many of them would be satisfied to achieve that goal alone. We must also develop in them the social, personal and life skills which will enable them to face the problem of unemployment and the possibility of long periods of free time. To quote the Scarman Report again:

"Children must be educated in the use of leisure. As time spent in working diminishes, the increased leisure must result not in boredom and idleness but in satisfying activity. Sport, the arts and recreational activity assume a great importance."

[8]

We are pleased to note that an increasing number of careers teachers see their task in this extended way. We would hope that the skills learned at school would enable young people to obtain their first jobs, develop their careers subsequently and find acceptance by society. Careers education can achieve much, but not in isolation: all teaching staff must appreciate the problems and there must be involvement across the curriculum.

Schools cannot work in isolation either. Links must be made with parents, as we have discussed in the previous section of this chapter. Many parents need to be helped to know more about the British education system and the complete range of opportunities available. They should be led to greater awareness of the careers service and all that it offers and of the roles of the careers officer and careers teacher. But if parents should know more about the schools and what they can offer, the schools should know more about the parents and their community. Here is another link to the first part of this chapter.

Liaison between schools and local employers can also help the specific problems of school leavers from minority-groups, in addition to the obvious help that it gives to all school leavers. Some employers are less aware than some schools of the problems faced by minority-group youngsters and especially of the implications (both good and bad) of a linguistically mixed background. In particular there are questions about the kind of language used in employers' interviews that are very similar to those we raised in Chapter 5 about the language of examinations.

The Institute of Careers Officers, in its evidence to what was then the Rampton Committee, said:

"West Indian youngsters, like their white peers, are individuals. Some are completely realistic; others reflect the low expectations some parts of society have of them and need to be encouraged to lift their sights; while another group aspire beyond their immediate job expectations. With all, careers officers do not concentrate on current attainment to the exclusion of future potential ...

"Careers officers must ensure individual clients have sufficient time and care devoted to them and that West Indians feel that the careers service is completely without prejudice. Careers officers must also continue to educate employers about their duties and responsibilities in a multi-ethnic society."

[9] page 57

We endorse these views and extend them to apply to the whole range of minority groups, as we do the Rampton recommendation *([9] page 57)* that there should be more careers officers drawn from ethnic minority groups. The arguments here, concerning both the need and the means of meeting it, are very similar to those, which we shall set out in the next chapter, concerning teachers. We also share Rampton's concern that careers officers from minority groups should not be forced or encouraged to specialise in working with young people from their own or other minority groups.

The "separate schools" debate

There has been considerable debate in some parts of the country about setting up separate schools for some minority communities who define themselves in terms of their religion. Some have already been set up, as either independent or as voluntary schools.

While we feel that the creation of such schools runs counter to our desire to see pupils of all backgrounds educated together, the existence of voluntary and independent schools run by the various denominations of the Christian and Jewish faiths makes it hard to deny similar aspirations on the part of other communities.

We see dangers in such a development. Consciously to establish what might be seen by some as ghetto schools, to appear deliberately to encourage cultural isolationism, to risk limiting the life-style and culture choices of the pupils who attend such schools could serve to grant recognition to the beliefs and customs of a community at the expense of the right of individual young people within it to have the width of personal choice that we would consider desirable. While admitting the tensions that are all too likely to arise when young people seek to exercise such choice outside the confines of their ancestral culture, we assert their right to do so, and to have access to the educational background which will make such choice possible for them.

On the other hand we are forced to acknowledge the very real feeling on the part of some communities that their cultural and religious traditions are not ignored but positively discouraged in some schools which have not yet thought through the questions of pluralism and acceptance in the way we advocate. The curriculum of the school and its organisation and practices (some aspects of which are mentioned in this context in our Chapter 8) can all foster this feeling if they have not been adapted to suit the circumstances of a multi-cultural population.

So deep are the feelings in some minority communities that they have established independent schools working in highly adverse circumstances dictated by severe financial handicaps. We are concerned that, as a result, some of these schools provide an education that is woefully inadequate in almost every respect. Community willingness to accept such circumstances rather than participate in the maintained system reveals how far much of the latter falls short of meeting the needs of such communities.

79

The very separateness of these schools, especially when it is combined with this poor quality, is likely strongly to reinforce a ghetto mentality on the part of their pupils.

On the other hand we have come across other ethnic minority schools which are well provided for and deliver a very high quality of education.

The issue of voluntary schools for minority communities is one which has generated deep disagreement. Some people have vigorously defended the rights of any religious community to establish voluntary schools. Others, desperately concerned about the dangers of a ghetto approach, have joined the out-and-out secularists in demanding the total abolition of voluntary school status as the only way of removing what they see as a danger. The disagreement is revealed even within the Swann Committee. Its report states that independent schools lie outside its terms and hence it examines the issue only as it relates to voluntary schools:

"While we fully appreciate the concerns which have led some sections of the Asian Community to press for the establishment of their own schools, we do not believe that creating an artificially separate situation in which groups of children are taught exclusively by teachers from the same ethnic group is desirable from the point of view of the children, the minority community or society as a whole and we are not therefore convinced that 'separate' schools can be supported on these grounds .... Despite the clearly deeply felt case put forward by many community representatives in evidence to us, we consider that, on the basis of present evidence, the best and perhaps the only way of ensuring that ethnic minority communities in this country are able both to retain their religious, cultural and linguistic heritage, as well as being accorded full equality alongside members of the majority community, is within the broader pluralist context for which we have argued in this report. In many respects we feel that the establishment of 'separate' schools could well fail to tackle many of the underlying concerns of the communities and might also exacerbate the very feelings of rejection and of not being accepted as full members of society, which they were seeking to overcome."

[13] pages 509-510

This section of the Swann Report is accompanied by a note of dissent from six ethnic minority members of the Committee who, after acknowledging the other side of the case, argue:

"If and when Education for All is a reality there will be no need for separate schools. This is no reason however, for not considering the case at the present time.

"On the contrary, an emphasis on an ideal future may be an excuse for inaction in the present, and for failure to meet immediate needs.

"It may be impossible to make immediate and valuable progress towards Education for All if the case for voluntary schools is struck from the agenda.

"Finally, we emphasise that a number of separate schools would provide invaluable experience and evidence in the long journey towards the goal of Education for All which all members of the Committee seek."

[13] page 515

We find it impossible to come down unequivocally on either side of this debate. We do, however, urge that, where ethnic minority voluntary or independent schools exist, they should adopt the same cross-cultural perspectives (albeit from the basis of a firm grounding in their own culture) that we advocate for county schools. We believe that this is necessary for all pupils. It is implicit in this that the approach should extend to all schools, county, voluntary or independent (including the Christian denominational schools). To fail in this approach would, in our view, be a lamentable combination of isolationism and indoctrination. This needs to be examined by Her Majesty's Inspectorate when they look at voluntary and independent schools. A realisation in the education service of the multi-cultural nature of society has been a stated aim of Government since the 1977 Green Paper which we quoted in our opening chapter.

We also feel that the weight of minority-group opinion behind the desire for separate schools adds weight to our case for the reform of the whole education system in a pluralist, multi-cultural, anti-racist direction.

Summary of recommendations

6.1   We affirm the right of individuals to choose the extent to which they wish to associate themselves with their ancestral culture or with the one amidst which they live. We believe that schools should give their pupils the skills to make this choice available and the knowledge to make it informed.

6.2   To avoid this approach seeming to clash with family attitudes, close liaison between school and home is needed.

6.3   We agree that home visiting is essential but doubt whether the teaching profession is yet at a stage when all teachers can be effective in this role, especially when there is any width of cultural difference between the school and the host community.

6.4   We recommend wider use of home liaison teachers who are familiar with the languages of the locally significant minority communities.

6.5   Attention needs to be given to language of communication from the school or the education office to the home.

6.6   The time of entry to school is of vital importance for developing home/school links.

6.7   Teachers will better be able to understand pupils if they are aware of their background. Teachers from the host community will be helped in this if they can find opportunities for mixing socially in minority communities.

6.8   Schools should seek positive links with minority community activities aimed at complementing the school curriculum by teaching the children more about their ancestral culture. Schools should also be aware of the work of any supplementary schools in their area.

6.9   The education service should make more use of people from ethnic minorities in all areas of staffing and on governing bodies.

6.10 Schools should specifically teach the skills that are needed to apply for a job, and should also give their pupils the personal and life skills which will enable them, if necessary, to face the problem of unemployment.

6.11 Schools should help parents who themselves were educated elsewhere to understand the education system and job opportunities in Britain.

6.12 Schools have a role to play in helping employers understand the problems of young people from minority groups.

6.13 Where ethnic minority voluntary or independent schools exist they should adopt the same cross-cultural perspectives that we advocate for other schools.

Points for discussion

✳ How can each school develop the necessary links and sympathy with its local communities to make all the above possible?

✳ How can schools prepare pupils for the choice of life-style we describe if parents do not see this as desirable?

✳ How can we overcome the misunderstanding and hostility that exists between some minority-group parents and schools or the careers service?

✳ What should be the national policy about separate ethnic minority voluntary schools?

Chapter 7

Teacher education and recruitment

"...teachers are the key figures in the educational process and changes in classroom practice and in the overall ethos of schools depend to a very large degree on the co-operation and support of individual teachers."

[13] page 541

In this reference, the Swann Report recognises the very great responsibilities on teachers. Chapter 9 of that report, from which the above quotation comes, considers the questions of teacher education and the employment of ethnic minority teachers.

We believe that if the aims described in our preceding chapters are to be achieved there is need for a profound revision of thinking on teacher education. The need for this change was officially identified as long ago as 1981 in the Rampton Report. Since then there has been some progress, but nowhere near enough.

Change must begin in the schools themselves. The new curriculum approaches which we, and the Swann Report, advocate will give all young people, including those embarking on training as teachers, an increased awareness of the multi-cultural nature of society. One essential prerequisite for improving the supply of teachers from ethnic minorities (discussed later in this chapter) is for the schools' delivery of education to young people from these communities to become more effective, so that more of them reach qualification levels which will admit them to such courses.

Initial teacher training

None of the skills and levels of awareness that we have described in earlier chapters as being necessary for teachers in our multi-cultural society is likely to arise spontaneously. They all need
84

preparation, and new entrants to the profession are entitled to receive this preparation as an integral part of their initial training. Swann comments that:

"...attempts of the teacher training system over recent years to respond to the multi-cultural nature of society can perhaps best be seen as characterised by a confusion of aims and a lack of overall coherence."

[13] page 544

It is this coherence which must be seen as a priority. The DES must accept a share of blame. As late as 1971 it claimed that the percentage of newly qualified teachers who would teach in multi-racial schools was probably as low as 15% and training for all students to do so was impractical.

The James Report (1972) on teacher training took a wider view which we endorse:

"All students on initial or post-graduate courses can and should be made aware that wherever they teach, they will be doing so in a multi-cultural society."

[48]

It is not sufficient for training institutions to include in their courses an option or two about multi-cultural education. There has been some progress beyond this level of provision but not enough.

The Swann Report included a paper by Derek Cherrington and Ray Giles summarising the findings of a national survey (in 1979) of multi-cultural aspects of teacher training which found that in colleges and institutes of higher education,

"14 different colleges reported having a total of 26 different courses for multi-cultural education. Of these 26 courses only 4 were listed as compulsory. On the other hand there were 46 courses which were described as containing elements related to multi-cultural education. These were the combined offerings of 17 different colleges. Of these the majority were compulsory. It would appear that the majority of students and teachers following programmes offered through colleges which emphasise multi-cultural education, would receive it through compulsory offerings in the foundations and methods courses...It would also appear that the main thrust for development is coming from those colleges which are situated in or serve large urban conurbations."

[13] pages 616-617

The paper's findings in polytechnics were broadly similar, but of university Departments of Education it says:

"There were only 4 courses on multi-cultural education offered by 4 different universities. Only one (offered at Brunel) was designated as compulsory. There were also 13 courses identified as having elements related to multi-cultural education at 9 different institutions. Only 3 were designated as compulsory ...With some notable exceptions, there appear to be few obvious initiatives being taken in this sector of higher education."

[13] page 617

In 1984 a working party of the CNAA produced a discussion paper suggesting some principles which institutions could take into account in developing multi-cultural and anti-racist approaches within courses and their institutional context. The objective of this paper was:

"...permeation of all elements of initial or in-service courses with multi-racial and anti-racist considerations, including attitudes, skills and knowledge."

[49]

A resolution of AMMA Assembly in 1981 said, among other things, that the Association

"...believes that all student teachers in training ought to spend some time in a school with a multi-cultural population."

[50]

This view was echoed at about the same time by recommendation 50 of the report of House of Commons Home Affairs Committee *[10]* and later in the Swann Report *([13] page 565)*. Recently it has come to our notice that a number of training institutions without immediate local access to such opportunities for their students would like to develop links with areas where such opportunities could be provided, but are being prevented from doing so by the very significant costs involved. We would urge that funding should be made available for such schemes to go ahead.

In-service training

Of increasing importance is the recognition that initial training is indeed only a beginning. Induction and in-service training for experienced teachers are just as important. In the context of a profession whose numbers are diminishing, especially in the secondary sector, the proportion of the profession represented by new entrants will be small. Even if the limited progress mentioned above is greatly extended, the impact on the profession as a whole of more appropriate initial training will be limited.

We identify several different types of INSET that can make important contributions to attuning the education service to the needs of the multi-cultural society. All are necessary, alongside the reforms of initial training already mentioned, if the teaching profession is to bring itself to full readiness.

There is a need, to which many LEAs are beginning to respond, for specific courses on many aspects of multi-cultural and anti-racist education. These have an important role to play, but by their very nature will reach only the committed who are sufficiently aware of the needs to apply for such INSET. This has inherent dangers. A school may have one enthusiast who goes on such a course. This person is then labelled in the minds of colleagues as the "multi-cultural expert". To him will be referred everything from devising a special module in the curriculum to dealing with ethnic minority children who get into trouble. As a result, colleagues may end less involved in the relevant questions than was formerly the case. But to state the danger is not to decry the value of the courses.

The Swann report endorses a view quoted from our own earlier paper:

"In the same way that we believe that multi-cultural perspectives need to inhere in the whole of the school curriculum, they must inform a very wide spectrum of INSET, whatever its main purpose. Subject-based, pastoral and management courses all need to take account of how their own aspects of the education service need to respond to the issues of multi-cultural living. This is an important way of seeing that the approach we advocate really does begin to underpin the whole of the school, and also to reach the ears of some teachers who would not choose to go on the more specifically multi-cultural courses, in the hope of awaking their awareness."

[12] page 58, quoted in [13] page 583

Swann extends the concept of INSET in this field to cover teachers in all-white schools and reports that such provision is almost non-existent. The report says:

"It could be suggested that this gap in provision could be filled by a major extension of existing in-service courses to LEAs and teacher-training institutions in 'all-white' areas. This assumes however that the in-service needs of a teacher in an 'all-white' school are the same as those of a teacher in a multi-racial school, and...there are clear differences of emphasis and concern in these different contexts. We believe therefore that there is an urgent need to develop appropriate in-service courses across the range of provision...designed specifically to enable teachers from 'all-white' schools to incorporate a pluralist perspective in their work and to bring their pupils to a positive understanding and appreciation of the multi-cultural nature of society."

[13] page 589

We endorse this view.

The most productive form of INSET for developing a whole-school concept of the multi-cultural society is undoubtedly school-based INSET, which uniquely can influence a whole staff. The growth of awareness of the need for whole-school policies in this and other areas makes the school-based approach a natural one to adopt. The Swann Report, following the James Report and, in its own area of study, the Cockroft Report, says:

"School-based activities can be seen as the only effective means of influencing those teachers, who may have received their initial training the longest ago, and may therefore be most able to benefit from updating of their knowledge and skills, but are the least likely to attend an out-of-school in-service course although they may be in positions of authority within schools."

[13] page 593

Swann points out the value that "distance learning" techniques such as those pioneered by the Open University can have in a school-based programme. In this context we would particularly commend the package *Case studies in multi-cultural education* produced by the BBC in the form of ten training films *[39]* with accompanying book *[40]* and discussion notes.

As in so many things, what we advocate cannot be achieved without resources. In this case the most important resource is time for such school-based INSET to take place.

There is also considerable value in teacher exchange programmes. In the past the majority of these have involved British teachers exchanging with teachers in the countries of origin of their local minority groups. Swann rightly points out that the increase in the number of British-born ethnic minority pupils limits the value of this type of exchange. Instead the report advocates

"...teacher exchanges...*within this country* as part of broadening the horizons of all schools to appreciate the different perspectives and opportunities offered in multi-racial and 'all-white' schools for the development of an overall education process which seeks to prepare *all* pupils for life in a genuinely pluralist society."

[13] page 596

We applaud this suggestion.

The recent Home Office review of the use made by local authorities of Section 11 funding has led to a number of teachers being designated as having specific responsibilities in connection with minority-group pupils. We know that many of the teachers involved, especially in the primary sector, feel the need of INSET to put them in a position to discharge this newly designated responsibility.

Recruitment of teachers from ethnic minorities

Teachers from ethnic minorities are regrettably and evidently a minority in themselves. Ethnic minority representation in the teaching profession is considerably smaller (as a percentage) than in the population as a whole.

There are two main reasons why this is a cause for concern. One involves equitable treatment of these minority communities. Their under-representation in the teaching profession (and elsewhere) is evidence of deliberate or unconscious prejudice in selection procedures, of failure by the education service to deliver to them the qualifications obtained by their majority-group contemporaries, or both. This is cause for concern and ought to be remedied.

But this is not all. Ethnic minority members of the teaching profession, of other parts of the education service and of other caring professions, can contribute to the effectiveness of the service by their very presence, over and above their direct contribution in the exercise of their profession. Their existence and visibility make them role-models for their pupils (majority and minority alike), giving the lie to the stereotype that Individuals from minority groups can have only very limited educational targets.

The need for more of these teachers in schools with multi-ethnic populations is clear to most teachers who work in such establishments, but we believe that teachers from ethnic minorities should in no way be restricted to such schools. Not only would this be to treat them as less than fully equal to any other teachers, but it would also deny that they have a contribution to make in 'all-white' schools, where racial stereotypes may be in most need of challenging. On this point the Swann Report again quotes with approval our earlier document:

"…it could be argued that where a school, because of its mono-cultural population, has been slow to realise the need to take account of the multi-cultural nature of society outside the school, then the appointment to it of one or more teachers from ethnic minority groups may well be a useful catalyst. We are not arguing that teachers from minority groups are in any sense automatically experts in, or even enthusiasts for, the sort of multi-cultural approach that we advocate. Individuals may or may not be. What we do suggest is that the arrival of such a teacher in a previously mono-cultural school may cause white colleagues (and pupils) to ask some questions for the first time."

[12] page 59, quoted in [13] pages 604-605

The need to recruit more teachers from the ethnic minorities was clearly set out in the Swann Report (*[13], pages 601-605*), which also pointed out the need for statistical information about the existing distribution of ethnic minority members within the teaching force. Both of these needs have met with some response from the Government and elsewhere.

In July 1985 the DES issued two discussion papers, on the supply of ethnic minority teachers *[51]* and on the collection of ethnic statistics about teachers *[52]*. The latter was in response to specific recommendations in both the Rampton and Swann Reports that such statistics should be collected about pupils, teachers and student teachers in training. There was already a DES working party in existence looking at the question of collecting these statistics about pupils and at this stage a parallel group was set up to consider a similar exercise for schoolteachers. This question will be discussed in more detail in Chapter 8.

The Commission for Racial Equality was at that time already engaged in a research project to analyse the incidence of ethnic-minority teachers in a sample of LEAs and their distribution among the various levels of promotion. It is anticipated that the report of this research is likely to be published at around the same time as this paper.

CRE also organised two seminars, *Black teachers: where they are in the system* (June 1985) and *Black teachers: the challenge of increasing the supply* (October 1986). The writing of the current section of this paper has been heavily influenced by participation in these two seminars. The seminars identified a number of reasons which limit the recruitment of black teachers and went some way to indicating how some of them might be overcome.

The whole question of recruitment methods and procedures is crucial. Many aspects, such as the choice of where to advertise posts, word-of-mouth soliciting of applications and the encouragement of applications from within the existing work-force, while not discriminatory in intent, in practice tend to perpetuate existing imbalances in the composition of that force. This tendency, an excellent example of what is described as "institutional racism", can be overcome only by careful attention to recruitment procedures and targeting of advertising to reach more ethnic-minority aspirants.

The wording of advertisements and job-descriptions and the attitudes of even the most well-meaning of interviewers often disguise quite unrealised assumptions and norms which create hidden barriers for candidates from ethnic-minorities. Here the remedies lie with scrupulous attention (with appropriate advice) to the wording of advertisements and job descriptions and the provision of training in bias-free interviewing techniques for selectors. One of the problems here is that in many LEAs the responsibility for teaching appointments (especially at senior level) lies with lay governors and elected LEA members who could be offered such training but cannot be compelled to take it. Nevertheless access to such training for these people is essential along with compulsory training for head teachers and LEA inspectors/advisers who share the responsibility of appointments, whether as full participants or in an advisory role.

There is evidence of the existence of one considerable untapped pool of potential teachers from ethnic-minorities in the form of people with overseas qualifications which are not recognised by the DES as adequate for qualified teacher status. This situation was revealed by the first of the two CRE seminars. As a result, the DES has begun a cautious overhaul of the system of recognition of such qualifications. This has not yet reached the point where the criteria on which such judgements are made have been made available for public comment: it is to be hoped that this step will not be long delayed. There are significant numbers of people in this country, mainly within the various Asian communities, with teaching experience in their countries of origin and overseas qualifications such as two first degrees, one in a subject and one in education, who cannot obtain DES recognition of these even for admission to a PGCE course.

One possible course of opening up a channel for such people to enter the teaching profession is by topping-up courses designed to overcome the DES-perceived deficiencies in the courses previously taken and bring their level of qualification up to what the Department is prepared to recognise for qualified teacher status. Ideas such as a shortened two-year BEd course have been mooted and some progress made, but there are problems of funding (both of the course and of individual students) and of local access that can be overcome only if both central and local Government make a conscious commitment to them.

Special access courses, often targeted at particular groups, with the aim of providing a route into professional training (not only for teaching) for those without the conventional entry qualifications, have existed for some time, partly in response to a DES initiative of 1978. In our previous publication we said:

"The Rampton Report and the Home Affairs Committee both recommended that such provision should be extended and that the availability of grants for students on such courses should be improved. We support such an extension with one important proviso. The purpose of such courses is to bring the students concerned up to the normal level of qualification for entry to teacher training, not to provide an easy entry at a lower level of qualification. This we believe to be integral to the whole idea. If it were not so, then the process would be self-defeating as an attempt to raise the perceived status of members of minority groups. The creation of a class of 'second-class' teachers from ethnic-minorities would indeed be an evil. Further, we believe that even a suspicion that this was what access courses were doing would be a grave danger, not only to the status of those who enter the profession by this route, but also to that of teachers from minority groups who enter teaching through the traditional route.

"One way which we have suggested that such access courses could be made visibly to adhere to their proper purpose is to avoid any blurring of the boundary between the access course and the training course it feeds, with a clear qualification at the end of the access course which is assessed and administered separately from the subsequent course."

[12] pages 59-60

We have had no cause to change our view on this point and have been encouraged to hear that some access courses are developing in the way we suggest, with a qualification at the end which has recognisable market value, partly in order to qualify for

93

the DES criteria for "normal" entry to teacher training, a category that the DES insists should take up at least 75% of the places on each initial training course.

Whatever steps are taken to increase the recruitment of teachers from minority groups, they will be severely hampered by the low public esteem in which the profession is currently held. Many black people have experienced forms of discrimination that have made them particularly aware of social status. While teachers as a group are seen as having a low status, black people will find this even more of a disincentive than do their white contemporaries to joining the profession.

Problems faced by black teachers

One of the major factors which limits the numbers of teachers from ethnic minorities is the very real problems facing many of those who do join the profession, especially those who are visibly easily recognised as belonging to minority groups. As was said in evidence given to the Swann Committee by the CRE:

"What is most apparent ... is the widespread sense of frustration and bitterness among ethnic minority teachers about what they see as their subordinate and disadvantaged position in the teaching profession."

[13] page 602

The Swann Report itself comments:

"Although evidence of actual discrimination is hard to come by, it is clear that ethnic minority teachers have been and are still subject to racism both in gaining employment and in advancing their careers. On our own visits to schools we have been concerned at the number of fully qualified ethnic minority teachers whom we have met who are 'stagnating' in the system, in posts far below their capabilities and experience. A matter of even greater concern is the number of ethnic minority teachers who, discouraged and disenchanted with the obstacles which they feel have been placed in the way of their progress in the teaching profession, have turned to other forms of employment."

[13] page 602

The evidence for how prejudice works against black teachers

is by its nature anecdotal, but we believe it to be thoroughly predictable that statistical evidence for its effect will come out of the CRE research project referred to above and the statistical monitoring of the teaching force being conducted by some LEAs. We have every reason to believe that the few black people currently in the teaching profession are disproportionately represented on the lower salary scales and on temporary contracts. Many of them, therefore, are in highly vulnerable positions when questions of redeployment or redundancy arise.

A very significant proportion of black teachers are in posts (such as ESL and mother-tongue teaching posts) which many people (wrongly in our view) regard as marginal to the profession. Certainly such posts are not ones from which it is at all easy to progress to senior positions within schools. Furthermore we have heard of cases where black teachers have been persuaded (possibly by a feeling that this was the only promotion open to them) to accept posts funded from Section 11 with very artificial job-descriptions. In some cases not only are the teachers concerned perceived as being on the fringes of the profession but are also prevented from developing and exercising their talents in the mainstream of teaching.

This is not only unjust to the teachers concerned, it also affects the perception of the potential of such teachers by colleagues, governors, LEAs, parents and pupils, hence reinforcing the cycle of injustice. To black pupils it has a heavily negative effect on their view of teaching as a possible career.

Many black teachers feel, not without reason, that in order to compete successfully for initial appointments and subsequent promotion in an increasingly competitive market, they need to have a substantially higher level of qualification than their white counterparts. This is part of a general problem facing black people seeking employment. The experience of black teachers arriving for interview to find a clear change of apparent attitude when a British-sounding name is seen to go with a black face is commonplace. In extreme cases interviewers have found it difficult to believe that the black candidate is a genuine candidate for the post. This is, of course, not restricted to the teaching

95

profession or to black people. At AMMA's conference *Positive and negative discrimination in multi-cultural Britain [53]*, Jocelyn Barrow, an experienced and respected teacher-trainer and a governor of the BBC, told us how frequently on arriving somewhere for a meeting she is mistaken for the tea-lady.

Black teachers do not always feel at home in predominantly white staff-rooms. While this may at times be because of deliberate and malicious prejudice, more often it is caused by a lack of ease on the part of white colleagues towards somebody they see (literally) as "different". This leads to what can seem (even if it is not intentionally) a closing of the ranks against the minority group. The same effect can give white teachers better access in practice to senior colleagues. This can become a self-reinforcing spiral.

Black teachers who, rarely, achieve a senior post are in a vulnerable position. They can be the target of distrust and even abuse from inside and outside the education service on the part of the directly prejudiced. At the same time they are vulnerable to accusations by their black colleagues of "selling out". They need particular support.

Many white heads, on the other hand, in part because of a lack of awareness of the specific problems faced by black teachers, fail to act sensitively and supportively when members of their staff encounter such problems.

There are many aspects of criticism that are directed both at black teachers and at white, such as incompetence, over-reaction and a whole range of professional failings. When such an accusation is levelled at a black teacher, it is hard for them in the context of prejudice which is their daily experience to distinguish whether this is a legitimate complaint, an instance of racial prejudice or the sort of unjustified grumble that can be aimed at any colleague, black or white.

Teachers, no less than children, need to be motivated. Therefore if black teachers feel that they have been pre-judged and relegated to an inferior position they lose the drive to give of their best, to their detriment and that of the service. Some possible ways of combating the forms of individual and institutional racism which give them this feeling will be considered in Chapter 8.

Summary of recommendations

7.1 There should be a multi-cultural, anti-racist core to all initial teacher training, which should include a grounding in awareness of and sensitivity to language.

7.2 All student teachers in training should spend some time in a school with a multi-cultural population.

7.3 There is a need for specific INSET courses on aspects of multi-cultural and anti-racist education, but these elements should also underpin a very wide spectrum of other INSET.

7.4 School-based INSET and distance-learning techniques can contribute to the development of whole-school multi-cultural and anti-racist approaches.

7.5 There is serious under-representation of ethnic minorities in the teaching profession. Ways must be found of overcoming this.

7.6 It would be wrong to try to attract more teachers from minority groups by lowering the standards for entry to the profession.

7.7 The DES should review and publish its criteria for recognition of overseas qualifications.

7.8 Topping-up and special access courses should be given more encouragement and the courses and students adequately funded.

7.9 Special access courses should lead to a clear qualification, assessed and administered separately from the training course into which the access course feeds.

7.10 Methods of recruitment should be freed from bias.

7.11 Black teachers need support in the face of prejudice from some colleagues, superiors, pupils and parents. Those in senior positions have particular needs in this respect.

Points for discussion

✱ How can a school avoid the danger that any matter (or pupil) labelled "multi-cultural" is ignored by the rest of the staff after referral to the teacher who has been on a course?

* How can initial teacher education and INSET be reformed to meet the targets we have described?

* How can we attract more members of ethnic minorities to apply for teacher training?

* How can we eliminate the prejudice shown towards teachers from ethnic minorities? How can we support them in the face of such prejudice?

Chapter 8

Anti-racist strategies

Strategies in schools and colleges

Chapter 4 discussed how the formal curriculum of a school can acknowledge the multi-cultural nature of society. We have earlier expressed the view that such a multi-cultural curriculum must lie at the centre of any long-term programme to combat racism, but that there are also urgent short-term needs that require other strategies.

The Swann Report quoted an Asian fifth-former:

"… I attended a middle school where approximately 90% of the pupils were white. The results of this situation were terrifying. The group of black children was bussed to school and then isolated from their neighbourhood. At home they were again isolated from any school contacts. During the four years I spent in that school, not one person attended any after-school activities for fear of walking through the neighbourhood where about 92% of the population were white. It would be literally true to say there was a physical barrier between our homes and our school and the only way in or out was on the coach. At school the situation was the same. The Asians were constantly in fear of being attacked by the several gangs of white boys. As we ran towards the staff room a teacher would come out and disperse the white gang, throw us back into the playground and then walk back as if nothing had happened. The teachers had no idea of what we were experiencing."

[13] pages 34-35

Here we see racial harassment in the outside community and in the playground. The teachers seem either unaware or unconcerned, an attitude which, although not racist in intention, is inevitably perceived as condoning racism. One might ask whether this is an isolated case or symptomatic of a pattern. For evidence of the prevalence of racial harassment we refer to the Home Office Study Group report which we have already quoted in a different context in Chapter 2:

"In all the places we visited, we were given accounts of racial violence, abuse and harassment … Assaults, jostling in the streets, abusive remarks, broken windows, slogans daubed on walls – these were among the less serious kinds of harassment which many members of the ethnic minorities (particularly Asians) experience, sometimes on repeated occasions. The fact that they are interleaved with far more serious racially-motivated offences (murders, serious assults, systematic attacks by gangs on people's homes at night) increases the fear experienced by the ethnic minorities. … Even in places where comparatively few racial incidents have occurred, the awareness of what is happening in other parts of the country induces a widespread apprehension that the climate locally is likely to deteriorate and that more serious incidents are likely in the future."

[19]

This fear is part of the daily experience of very many ethnic minority youngsters in our schools who may themselves be subjected to such incidents in and out of school, and will certainly be aware of many more such incidents involving their friends and relations. One cannot be surprised that many ethnic minority communities acquire from this a heightened awareness of the threat of racial harassment, which in turn leads them to a sensitivity towards any hint of racial bias which could seem exaggerated to a white person who did not understand the context.

Clearly one of the first priorities for a school is to do all that it can to prevent such incidents within its own walls. This requires a clear policy and set of procedures. To treat a racially motivated attack as just another fight is not enough: the motivation must be dealt with as well as the form through which it is expressed, and any incident with racist overtones should be treated considerably more seriously than if such overtones had been absent.

One of the most difficult tasks that classroom teachers have to tackle is that of mediation in relationships between pupil and pupil.

The task is particularly difficult in some schools, mainly secondary, where overt aggression between pupils of different backgrounds arises, in circumstances no different from those of incidents between pupils of the same group. Often the aggression is verbal and the aggressor may well not intend anything more than a momentary effect. The victim, however, may regard the abuse as racist and evidence of a longer-term wish to victimise. The situations that such episodes can lead to are not easy to handle, and are even more difficult when there are genuinely racist intentions.

Verbal abuse and graffiti involving racial language are, alas, very common indeed. Whatever the intention, all of it is likely to wound. Schools and colleges should be aware of this and treat it seriously. Use of the language of racial abuse creates a climate which gives strong messages of rejection to pupils (and staff) from ethnic minorities. If it appears to go unchallenged by the institution, this leads them to think that the abuse is tolerated, even encouraged. Furthermore, such a climate can pave the way for more serious incidents.

While very few teachers are likely to tolerate the more blatantly abusive language ("nigger" and "coon"), not enough are sensitised to other words such as "paki" which can wound just as much. Further, the fashion in racial abuse changes and teachers must be on the look-out for the new cuss-words. The use of such language by pupils or colleagues, whether in malice or more casually, should always be challenged. A clear school policy and procedure are needed. Some teachers, often but by no means exclusively the less experienced, find it hard to talk to pupils about such matters, and clear policy and procedure will help to overcome this barrier.

For more serious racial offences, serious measures are appropriate, at times to the level of expulsion. This requires a realisation of the seriousness of such offences shared not only by the staff but also by the governing body. Recent cases, notably that of Poundswick High School in Manchester, have unfortunately shown that without LEA backing even unanimity between staff and governors is not sufficient.

As well as dealing with individual incidents, teachers should be on the look-out for patterns of behaviour in individuals or groups which might indicate grounds for more serious concern about the attitudes held. Some schools have introduced a system of logging any incidents with obvious or suspected racial motivation so that senior staff can monitor whether individual pupils feature disproportionately either as perpetrators or as victims.

It is unfortunately true that very often children bring racist attitudes to school with them from home. Here too the school has a part to play. A policy that, following any racially motivated incident, the offender's parents are seen by senior staff produces a double benefit. Where school and parents agree about the unacceptable nature of the offence, they can work together. Where the parents themselves exhibit racial prejudice, to make the school's disapproval clear to them may not necessarily cause them to modify their views but will be an influence to moderate their expression of those views.

One symptom of racial problems of which teachers should be aware is the existence in a multi-racial school of strongly knit peer-groups from a single ethnic group, white or black. These in themselves impose a limitation on the social experience of their members. They are often seen by teachers as quite natural and nothing to worry about, but very often their existence is a defence mechanism which should be seen as evidence that something is wrong. If the composition of the peer-groups in a school is dominantly racial, this indicates that somewhere in those children's experience there is likely to be some form of racial pressure against which they are seeking each other's support. It is important to watch for such symptoms, since in many cases the victims of racial harassment are reluctant to broach the subject with their teachers, either out of fear of reprisal or because they see little hope in avoiding the inevitable. In some cases it is likely to be because they do not expect sympathy or understanding from white teachers.

It may well be argued that racist attacks tend to happen outside schools and colleges much more than inside and that therefore the institution can do nothing. While the premise is probably correct, the conclusion does not follow. The attitude shown by the institution can be either dismissive of the problem or concerned about it and supportive of the victims and their community. The choice of attitude will be very influential in determining the extent to which ethnic minority pupils can identify themselves as members of the school or college community and hence of their motivation in all aspects of school or college life. The institution needs to be aware of the tensions and pressures in its local community and when harassment occur to pupils, even if totally outside the school or college, to support the victims and to make it quite clear to perpetrators and the wider community that racial harassment is something of which the school or college community very firmly disapproves.

Where, as sometimes happens, the climate of racist attacks outside is brought on to the school site by intruders, the school has an opportunity, and an obvious responsibility, to make its attitude doubly clear, to victims and offenders, in the way it handles the incident.

Most perpetrators of racist attacks are of an age which means that either they are still at school or they have not long left. It follows that to the extent that schools are successful in encouraging better attitudes towards minority groups, the prevalence of such incidents is likely to decrease. The fostering of attitudes is something that the school needs to do in a number of ways through its academic, pastoral and hidden curricula. Part of the process is the teaching of good manners: sensitivity to other people and that, for example, names can wound. This can and must start at a very early age.

It is also necessary that pupils learn about the nature and mechanisms of group prejudice (applied to race, gender and to other groupings). This ought to come at some stage in the formal curriculum, probably at secondary level when children are more likely to benefit from the approach of "knowing the enemy". It could be covered through the medium of history, social studies, religious studies, life skills or literature and probably other subjects as well. The subject label does not matter as long as the topic is covered, for all pupils and as soon as they are able to appreciate the concepts. Schools should check to see that this really does happen and that this important topic is not left in the gaps between subjects with everybody assuming it is somebody else's job to teach it.

We have already discussed the multi-cultural approach to the curriculum which we advocate for all schools, but in that discussion (Chapter 4) we confined ouselves to the overt, formal curriculum. The true curriculum is the whole set of experiences that the child receives in school. The hidden curriculum is possibly even more important for our purposes than the overt one. Whatever subject is taught and whatever classroom materials are used, teachers' attitudes to pupils are seen in their actions and speech directed towards (or away from) such pupils. We believe that there will be little advantage in promoting curricular and other changes in schools if no attempt is made to foster the personal relationships which are the basis of the attitudes so many children have to their schools and learning.

Relationships between pupils and teachers depend on mutual respect. Teachers will be better able to understand pupils if they are familiar with the background from which the children come, with the values, assumptions and aspirations of that culture. Thus they will more readily comprehend difficulties the children might encounter in finding their feet in society. This understanding cannot come from reading alone since cultural differences often show themselves in ways scarcely recorded. There is, for example, a particular kind of smile displayed by many people of Afro-Caribbean background as a response indicating embarrassment: it looks very like the response used by white children to indicate contempt or insolence. A teacher unaware of the difference will obviously be liable to make serious errors in interpreting pupils' behaviour.

Teachers are obvious role-models for their pupils and must be very self-critical to ensure that they live up to the standards they set, not only in the more obvious ways such as use of language, but in avoiding subtler, possibly unconscious forms of bias and stereotyping. The latter are often much more noticeable to the victim than to the often unwitting perpetrator. This does require a considerable level of individual and group self-awareness. A strong consensus among the staff as a body will help. Not only will it keep the well-intentioned up to the standards to which they aspire, but it will also influence the less well-intentioned into at least moderating their practice if not actually modifying their attitudes.

There is a whole area of school routine that can lead to clashes with minority cultures if not handled sensitively. Such aspects as school uniform, meals, physical education (particularly for girls from some Asian cultures) and the observance of religious fasts can too often lead to incidences of institutional racism. For a school to take firm, insensitive attitudes in cases where such matters conflict with the practice of minority groups can become racism by effect, which is all too easily perceived as racism by intention. Some of the problems which occur in this way are easily solved, given an open and accepting attitude by the school. Others are less tractable and need to be talked through very carefully and sensitively with parents either individually or as a group. It is friction over matters of this kind which often fuels the wish on the part of some minority groups to set up their own schools.

In all the matters we have dealt with in this chapter and others it is not enough for schools to make appropriate policy statements unless they also take steps to see that these policies are effectively delivered. To do this requires a continuous process of monitoring within the school. Appendix 3 contains a check-list of questions for schools designed to help with such monitoring. We believe that each school should maintain such a check-list and should use it regularly to evaluate its practices. This process needs to involve the whole staff but appropriate senior staff should have the responsibility, written into their job-description, of taking the lead. To perform this function the school will need to know the ethnic composition of its own population. The use of ethnic statistics will be considered in the last part of this chapter.

Strategies at LEA level
Every LEA has two areas of responsibility which are relevant to the multi-cultural society: as a part of the eduction service and as an employer.

Educationally they should have policies to foster in their schools and colleges the kinds of curriculum and attitudes we have described in earlier chapters. Although curriculum is ultimately the responsibility of heads and their staffs, there is much that the LEA can do to encourage and support a multi-cultural approach.

A large proportion of LEAs have appointed inspectors or advisers with specific responsibility for multi-cultural or anti-racist education. These are largely in places where the presence of significant ethnic-minority populations makes the needs obvious. Our belief that a multi-cultural perspective should underpin the curriculum for *all* pupils implies that every LEA should make such appointments in order to support schools in their development of multi-cultural and anti-racist approaches. These specific posts are not enough. Just as multi-cultural approaches need to be inherent in the whole curriculum, so they need to pervade all parts of the LEA inspectorate/advisory service.

Many aspects of education need suitable provision if they are to respond adequately to the needs of a multi-cultural society. The need for ESL and mother-tongue teachers (whether in mainstream schools and colleges, in special centres or in adult education), for home-school liaison teachers with appropriate facility in the languages of the local community and of bilingual teachers (especially for the youngest pupils) will vary from one LEA to another and locally within each LEA. To make the proper provision the LEA must know its global and local needs, which again links to the question of the use of ethnic statistics.

The school meals service will need to be aware of the numerical strength, school by school, of those minority communities with particular dietary practices.

The LEA library service will need to take account in its acquisition policy of the local pattern of minority languages. It should also provide for teachers materiographies and sample collections of learning materials to support a multi-cultural approach. While the amount of suitable materials available from the major eductional publishers has improved considerably in recent years, many people working in this field still see considerable need to use specialist publishers whose output might not be so well known unless specifically brought to teachers' attention.

LEAs are major providers of in-service training and should see that their provision meets the criteria we have described in Chapter 7. Where the LEA also runs one or more colleges providing initial training then it has equivalent responsibilities there.

In appointing governors to its schools and colleges, the LEA ought to ensure that significant minority communities obtain adequate representation. The routine of relying on political parties' local organisations to achieve this will almost certainly not have the desired effect.

As an employer, the LEA has a legal duty to operate even-handedly between the different ethnic groups (as indeed it must between the sexes). It should have an equal opportunities policy. The Commission for Racial Equality has published a Code of Practice under the Race Relations Act 1976 [3]. The purpose and status of this Code are described in its own opening paragraphs:

"1.1 This Code aims to give practical guidance which will help employers, trade unions, employment agencies and employees to understand not only the provisions of the Race Relations Act and their implications, but also how best they can implement policies to eliminate racial discrimination and to enhance equality of opportunity.

"1.2 The Code does not impose any legal obligations itself, nor is it an authoritative statement of the law – that can only be provided by the courts and tribunals. If, however, its recommendations are not observed this may result in breaches of the law where the act or omission falls within any of the specific prohibitions of the Act. Moreover its provisions are admissable in evidence in any proceedings under the Race Relations Act before an Industrial Tribunal and if any provision appears to the Tribunal to be relevant to a question arising in the proceedings it must be taken into account in determining the question. If employers take the steps that are set out in the Code to prevent their employees from doing acts of unlawful discrimination they may avoid liability for such acts in any legal proceedings brought against them."

[55] page 4

The Code indicates the responsibilities of employers under the Act, shows how their implementation ties in with good employment practice and indicates the elements that need to be present in an equal opportunities policy.

It is our belief, following the provisions of this Code, that the proper operation of such a policy requires the LEA to have monitoring processes (including statistical monitoring) to assess its success in fulfilling such a policy and the directions in which change is needed. Since the publication of the Code in 1983 and its adoption by Parliament in the following year, a number of LEAs have responded to it by introducing such a monitoring process. AMMA has issued advice to branch secretaries about criteria to apply in local negotiations over such an introduction.

The LEA should see that its procedures for appointment and promotion of staff are as free from overt or hidden bias as can be arranged and provide training in bias-free interview techniques for all staff involved in interviewing and as many school and college governors as can be persuaded to take up such training.

We believe that to redress the undoubted historic imbalance in employment of ethnic-minorities in teaching and other professions requires positive action. Even when all the procedures surrounding the appointment and promotion of staff have been examined and freed from conscious or unconscious bias, there will still be a need to attract more ethnic-minority members into applying for responsible posts. To say this is not to advocate the idea of employment quotas in any section of the service. In any case, such quotas are illegal. There is much that can be done, for example, to target advertising, not least by using the minority-community press as well as the more traditional media for job advertisements.

Teachers and support staff are not always blameless of overt

108

racial prejudice and even, at times, of harassment. When this occurs in the course of somebody's work then it is a form of unprofessionalism and a legitimate cause for disciplinary complaint and action by the employer. Some LEAs in recent years have introduced their own codes of conduct or policy statements about dealing with racism on the part of teachers and other employees. Others have simply inserted into existing disciplinary and/or grievance procedures sentences to make it clear that racial and sexual harassment come within the scope of such procedures. We believe that such misconduct is implicitly covered by such procedures in any case, but welcome its being made explicit. We strongly prefer an arrangement in which these particular forms of misconduct are dealt with through existing negotiated disciplinary procedures rather than through a separate system.

In particular we deplore the excessive zeal of some LEAs and some officers of others who operate as though the most minor allegation of racism is conclusive proof of major misconduct, exempt from all normal rules of evidence or fair hearing. This attitude is unjust to the employees accused. It also exhibits anti-racism in a bad light, discourages those who are unsure about it and disadvantages the very groups it is intended to help by making a racist backlash all too likely.

On the other hand we also deplore those attitudes of some heads and LEA officers who appear consistently to dismiss as trivial any allegation of racial discrimination that is brought before them.

There are times when a racist organisation in the wider community singles out for a campaign of vilification a school with a high proportion of ethnic-minority pupils and a particularly strong anti-racist stance. At such times active support from the LEA is essential and has, in those cases of which we are aware, usually been delivered willingly. One tactic which is often used by such organisations is to book the school hall for a meeting. While this does not formally constitute a public attack on the school it does give a strong message to the school community. If the school and LEA do not make their anti-racist stance absolutely clear and firm

109

they risk the dangers of guilt by association and the undermining of their position in the local community. It hardly needs saying that such abuse of school premises should not be allowed, and indeed we are aware that most, if not all, LEAs have rules which try to prevent it. But vigilance is essential. It is not unknown for racist organisations to book the use of the premises under the name of an individual for some quite different ostensible purpose, in which case the true nature of the meeting may emerge only at the time of the meeting itself.

Racist organisations are familiar with and make use of the legal rights of candidates in parliamentary or local elections. In these circumstances there is almost nothing that the school or LEA can legally do to prevent the use of the school hall for what is claimed to be an election meeting. Even if the declared public nature of the meeting is suspected of being totally bogus, this can only be proved in retrospect. The legal position was recently confirmed in a High Court judgment against ILEA over such a meeting at John Scurr School in Tower Hamlets. It is our view that the relevant legislation should be amended to prevent this sort of abuse. If the only way in which this can be done is to stop all election meetings from taking place on school premises then we do not believe that this is too high a price to pay.

The collection and use of ethnic statistics

In 1981 the Rampton Report's recommendations included the following:

"With effect from 1 September 1982:
(i)   All schools should record the ethnic origin of a child's family, along with the normal standard data when a child first enters school, on the basis of discussion with parents.
(ii)   The DES should reincorporate the collection of information on the ethnic origin of all pupils in schools into its annual statistical exercise and should introduce ethnic classifications into its school leavers survey.
(iii)   The DES should ask all teacher training institutions to collect statistics on the ethnic origin of students training to be teachers including students seeking to enter teaching

110

through special access courses.

(iv)   The DES should record and publish statistics on the ethnic origin of all teachers in employment by amending teachers' service cards to include information on ethnic origin.

(v)   The DES should arrange for the annual collection of details from all universities, polytechnics and colleges of higher education, of the ethnic breakdown of their student populations and should examine the reasons for any under-representation of any group at any institution."

[9] page 67

Shortly after publication of this report, the Home Affairs Committee recommended *[10]* that local authorities with significant ethnic-minority populations should institute ethnic monitoring of the services which they provide. The recommendation concerning teachers was echoed in the CRE Code of Practice:

"1.33 It is recommended that employers should regularly monitor the effects of selection decisions and personnel practices and procedures in order to assess whether equal opportunity is being achieved.

"1.34 The information needed for effective monitoring may be obtained in a number of ways. It will be best provided by records showing the ethnic origins of existing employees and job applicants."

[55] page 18

These recommendations in the Rampton Report proved highly controversial and produced no immediate action from the DES, although some monitoring by LEAs (much of it outside the education service) did begin in response to the CRE Code.

AMMA, in *Our multi-cultural society: the educational response [12],* set itself firmly in favour of such monitoring with appropriate safeguards to help allay the understandable fears of minority groups about abuse of such information.

In 1985 the Swann report *[13]* reaffirmed the Rampton recommendations on this subject. Shortly afterwards the DES established a working group to look at the value and practicality of collecting ethnically based statistics about school students. In the course of time it made its report *[53]* to the Secretary of State (at

111

that time Sir Keith Joseph) and in July 1986 his successor made an announcement in the Commons *[16]* accepting the main proposals of that report. These were:

✴ That he should urge LEAs to collect data about their pupils.

✴ This data should cover family origin (a set of categories was provided, but these could be further sub-divided if locally appropriate), language and religion.

✴ The data should be collected by schools from parents at the time of each child's beginning school or transferring between schools, as part of the routine collection of information that happens at such times. (In this the working party followed an earlier AMMA recommendation.)

✴ Data on named individuals should not pass outside the school, but aggregated statistical data should be passed to the LEA.

✴ There should be local consultations about such matters as confidentiality and security of the data.

Shortly before this group reported a second group was set up to look at similar questions about ethnically based statistics about teachers. At the time of writing this group is consulting about its draft report and hopes to present its final report to the Secretary of State early in 1987.

There are a number of different reasons why data about the ethnic origins of pupils, teachers and student teachers in training need to be collected at different levels in the education service.

On the whole we agreed with much of the report of the earlier of the two DES working groups which said:

"If schools and individual teachers are to be able to teach pupils effectively they have to know something about their backgrounds and the experiences they bring to school. For children entering school have already begun acquiring knowledge, beliefs, assumptions and a whole cultural and linguistic frame of reference. They will learn best if the teaching they receive is related to, and seeks to draw and build upon what they already know...

"If it is objected that teachers do not need formally to collect such information, we would point out that there are dangers involved in a teacher making assumptions about children's ethnic origins ... We suspect in any case that parents would be uneasy if they thought that teachers were operating on the basis of hunches, not facts. And even where individual teachers are well-informed, a general picture of the whole school's ethnic make-up may still be lacking. The purpose of having each school collect ethnically based data on each of its pupils is to bring together in a systematic, aggregated form information about the pupil body. From this more accurate base properly informed decisions can be taken about the provision the school should make ... It will also make schools better able to monitor the impact of their procedures and policies on different groups of children, correlating ethnically based data with other school data. ... Finally, the collection of ethnically based data would, by the same token, enable a school which felt that it was not receiving needed support from its LEA to present less impressionistic and hence more cogent arguments for new forms of provision or a change of approach."

[54] §§3.4-3.6

"We do not believe that it is possible for an LEA to make effective and efficient provision unless it has accurate statistics on the ethnic backgrounds of the children for whom it is providing ... Without such statistics, LEAs will not be able to monitor the impact of their policies and procedures, and decisions about provision must necessarily be rather hit and miss ... Ethnically based statistics will help them to identify what the needs are and where, and to target resources accordingly. They will also help to guide the deployment of staff ... for example in work with bilingual pupils. ... So too local statistics would enable LEAs to present a more convincing case when seeking funds from central Government (for instance, under the Urban Aid Programme or Section 11 of the Local Government Act 1966) so as to make better provision for the pupils in their area."

[54] §§3.8-3.11

The working party did not conclude that the purposes served by national aggregation of these statistics were sufficient to outweigh the suspicion of such an aggregation expressed by many people in the minority communities. It therefore recommended a purely local collection on a mutually compatible basis. For our part we believe that the value of national aggregation of the statistics would have been more valuable than some members of the group were willing to concede.

Ethnicity is not a simple concept, and to describe pupils' ethnic backgrounds in a way that will adequately inform educational planning and monitoring requires more than one parameter. The ones suggested by the DES working group seem to us to be sensible. That group suggested collecting data on religion, language and family origin (the last on the basis of a classification based on that used by the CRE, but which could be further sub-divided if that was appropriate to local needs).

Confidentiality of the data and the restriction of access to those with legitimate purposes are important considerations which must be taken into account in order to minimise the chance of the data being abused. We believe that one important aspect of this should be that ethnic data about named individual pupils should not pass out of the school; all other levels of the system would handle purely statistical information. Here again we endorse the recommendation of the DES working party:

"The arrangements for ensuring the confidentiality of information relating to individuals must be seen to be watertight. But at the same time much of the point of collecting ethnically based statistics would be lost if the aggregated results were not accessible for proper purposes. Each local authority should consult interested parties in the community concerning the arrangements for ensuring confidentiality before embarking on the collection of statistics, and should issue a code of practice."

[54] Recommendation 6

The question of what categories should be used for classifying family origins is a difficult one that leads to much debate. Many alternative schemes of classification have been proposed: none is perfect. We believe that the search for an ideal classification is a fruitless process which can unduly delay the implementation of local schemes. The fact that the DES working party report sets out a scheme of broad categories with which local schemes are urged to be compatible should help avoid such delays.

The questions about collection of ethnic statistics about teachers and student teachers in training are rather different. In this case the main purpose of the collection would be to monitor employment practices, where several pieces of research have shown the predominant factor in discriminatory practice to be skin colour. This means that a simpler ethnic classification is relevant. There are those who argue that a simple black/white distinction is all that is necessary here. While we would not go this far, we do believe that very broad categories are appropriate.

In the cases of their employees it probably is necessary for LEAs to record centrally ethnic data about named individuals, so that the progress through the career structure of individuals from different ethnic backgrounds can be monitored to identify problem areas. This lends extra importance to questions of security, confidentiality and access only for proper purposes. A code of practice is essential.

The collection of such data needs to take two forms. Applicants for posts (whether initial appointments or promotions) can be asked to complete a section of the form giving their ethnic background. We believe that this is of great value since to monitor the ethnic profile of the applicants indicates whether any targeting of advertising is successful. To correlate an analysis of the whole field of applicants with the field of people actually appointed can point up any prejudicial effects of the appointments system. We believe that such data should be collected, but that the relevant section of the form should be a tear-off slip that is handled solely by the personnel department of the LEA and is not available to interviewers or those doing short-listing.

In addition to this entry-monitoring the LEA needs to know the ethnic composition of its existing work-force. This requires a once-for-all survey after which, if individual data are centrally recorded, the record can be updated by entry data and data on resignations, retirements and promotions within the LEA service. Such a once-for-all collection is a large task and has significant cost implications, but we think it an essential prerequisite for monitoring employment practices.

There is disagreement in the debate about such a one-off

exercise as to whether the data should be collected by a process of self-classification or by management-led collection. We are unequivocally on the side of self-classification as the only logical and just way of doing the job. But whichever method is chosen, or if elements of both are combined, then there is a need to persuade the employees concerned (the teachers) and the managers (heads and LEA officers) to participate willingly. This involves two stages.

The first is full negotiation with the relevant unions and associations of the scheme, its procedures, its built-in safeguards against abuse and the code of practice about future use of the data. This may well involve teaching and non-teaching unions within the LEA workforce. The second is a carefully planned and well timed publicity exercise to inform employees of the purposes of the scheme and the safeguards that have been built into it. The area is a sensitive one and people need to understand what is happening and to have their doubts and fears alleviated by careful explanation.

Summary of recommendations

8.1 Schools should do all they can to prevent racial incidents on their own premises and to be supportive to pupils who are victims of such incidents elsewhere.

8.2 Any incident involving racism should be treated more seriously than if that element had not been present. Schools should have clear policies and procedures for this.

8.3 Any use of the language of racial abuse should be challenged.

8.4 For more serious racial offences, serious measures are appropriate, at times to the level of expulsion. School staffs, governing bodies and LEAs should take a united view of this.

8.5 Teachers should be on the look-out for patterns of individual or group behaviour that might indicate racial harassment or tension.

8.6 Secondary schools should include in their curriculum specific teaching about the nature and mechanism of group prejudice.

8.7 Teachers must be very self-critical in order to eliminate any bias or stereotyping from their teaching and professional relationships.

8.8 Areas of school routine which risk clashing with minority group practices should be discussed sensitively with parents.

8.9 Schools should monitor their effectiveness in delivering anti-racist policies.

8.10 LEAs should foster in their school the kinds of curriculum and attitudes we describe. Every LEA should have one or more inspectors or advisers with specific responsibility for multi-cultural and anti-racist education.

8.11 LEAs should make adequate provision for ESL, mother-tongue maintenance and home liaison.

8.12 In appointing governors to its schools and colleges, the LEA ought to ensure that significant minority communities obtain adequate representation.

8.13 LEAs should have equal opportunities employment policies and should monitor their effectiveness.

8.14 The under-representation of ethnic minorities in the teaching profession should be combated by such means as bias-free procedures and interview techniques, and appropriate targeting of job advertisements. We do not support the idea of ethnic quotas.

8.15 Overt racial prejudice on the part of teachers or support staff is a breach of professionalism and should be dealt with through negotiated disciplinary procedures.

8.16 Schools and LEAs need to be aware of the danger of abuse of school premises by racist groups.

8.17 We support the collection of ethnic data about pupils and teachers. The data should be based on information collected from parents in the case of pupils and self-classification in the case of teachers.

8.18 Confidentiality of ethnic data about named individuals is of paramount importance. Such data about named pupils should not pass outside the school: about teachers it should be confined to the personnel department of the

LEA. The only information that should be passed outside these bounds is aggregated statistical data. Access to all such data should be controlled to prevent abuse.

Points for discussion

❋ How can teachers recognise occurrences of racial harassment if the victims are unwilling to talk about them?

❋ How can teachers become aware of hidden bias in their teaching and professional relationships?

❋ How should a school monitor the effectiveness of its anti-racist policy?

❋ How can an LEA's equal opportunities employment policy be made effective?

❋ How can ethnic data about pupils and teachers be collected in a fair and secure way?

❋ Who should have access to ethnic statistics about pupils and teachers and for what purposes? Should any summaries of such data be made public?

Chapter 9

Conclusion

"Colour is no longer an indication of national origin. Until this century most racial and religious groups remained concentrated in their homelands but today almost every country of the Commonwealth has become multi-racial and multi-religious. This change has not been without its difficulties, but I believe that for those with a sense of tolerance the arrival and proximity of different races and religions have provided a much better chance for each to appreciate the value of the others."

[56]

These words of Her Majesty the Queen in 1982 show a level of acceptance of the multi-cultural nature of society. This acceptance is not yet as widespread as we would wish. Nor is the realisation that the changed nature of society has important implications for the educational system. The continuing public debate, within the education system as well as in wider society, means that our previous publication [12] appeared, three years later, to be seriously out of date. In particular, questions of racism are more central to the public debate now than they were at that time.

Our original central theses remain unchanged. If our diverse society is to be a peaceful one then an understanding of the backgrounds of all groups in the UK must pervade the education of all pupils and, more specifically, must also pervade all courses of teacher training, whether initial or in-service. If this happens, then not only will members of minority groups find themselves able to avail themselves of educational opportunities on an equal footing with the host community, but the host community itself will be better, more appropriately educated. Children from ethnic minorities should have an education which will equip them to make informed choices about the extent to which their adult

119

life-style will draw upon their ancestral culture and on the host culture amidst which they find themselves.

Alongside the development, through the curriculum, of a multi-cultural, world perspective, there need to be various shorter-term measures to combat the immediate threats posed by racism, whether overt or institutional.

We believe that the conflict seen by many people between multi-cultural and anti-racist approaches to education is a false one. The two need to go together. Without immediate anti-racist strategies, ethnic minorities will not be able to take the first steps in overcoming the obstacles created by prejudice and the long-term aims of a multi-cultural curriculum will not be achievable. Without a multi-cultural curriculum to lay an improved foundation of thought for future generations, anti-racism will never have the chance to be more than a form of crisis-management.

Some of the things we have sugested require action by the Government, the LEAs, the teacher training institutions or some other bodies outside the schools, but the majority are rooted in the attitudes and practices of individual teachers and schools. This is what one would expect from an association of classroom teachers. The major contribution towards a multi-cultural curriculum and appropriate anti-racist strategies in education will come from teachers. They will need various types of outside help, but only they are at the point of delivery in the schools and colleges. They need an awareness of the issues involved. For some this will mean a big change, but we are pleased to learn from our members that over the last few years the awareness has begun to extend itself beyond those inner-city schools where it started.

We also believe that AMMA, along with other teachers' organisations, has a role to play in maintaining and disseminating that awareness. The various organisations specific to ethnic minority teachers have their own role, complementary to that of the recognised unions and associations rather than competitive with them. It is perhaps significant that in considering the membership of the DES working group on the collection of ethnic statistics about schoolteachers, the group's representatives from the teacher associations were among those who argued vehemently for specific representation there of black teachers' organisations. AMMA would welcome dialogue with these organistions.

We hope that this booklet will continue the work of its two predecessors in raising the awareness among teachers of the issues involved in multi-cultural and anti-racist education and. We hear from many colleagues whose awareness of the issues has been recently awakened and are conscious of their own need for help and advice on how to incorporate their new understanding into the practice of their schools. We hope that this booklet will indicate to them where they might look for such help. Others have not yet realised the issues at stake. We hope that such colleagues will read what we have to say and wake up to the multi-cultural realities that have to be acknowledged in Britain's educational system.

Appendix 1

Bibliography

[1]   Local Government Act 1966
[2]   Race Relations Act 1968
[3]   Race Relations Act 1976
[4]   *The problems of coloured school leavers*
        Report of the Select Committee on Race Relations and
        Immigration, 1969
[5]   *Education in schools: a consultative document*
        HMSO Cmnd 6869, 1977
[6]   *The West Indian community*
        Report of the Select Committee on Race Relations and
        Immigration, April 1978
[7]   *Education for a multi-cultural society*
        AMMA, 1981
[8]   *The Brixton disorders, 10-12 April 1981*
        Report of an inquiry by the Rt Hon Lord Scarman OBE
        HMSO Cmnd 8427, 1981
[9]   *West Indian children in our schools*
        Interim Report of the Committee of Inquiry into the
        Education of Children from Ethnic Minority Groups
        (The Rampton Report)
        HMSO Cmnd 8273, 1981
[10]   *Racial disadvantage*
        Report of the House of Commons Home Affairs
        Committee, Session 1980/81, Fifth Report
        HMSO HC 424–1
[11]   *The secondary school curriculum and examinations*
        Report of the Select Committee on Education, Science and
        the Arts, 1982
        HMSO HSC 116–1
[12]   *Our multi-cultural society: the educational response*

AMMA, 1983   ISBN 902983 27 X

[13]   *Education for all*
       Report of the Committee of Inquiry into the Education of
       Children from Ethnic Minority Groups
       (The Swann Report)
       HMSO Cmnd 9453, March 1985

[14]   *Education for all: a brief guide to the main issues of the*
       Report
       Lord Swann FRS FRSE
       HMSO, 1985   ISBN 0 11 270570 7

[15]   Statement by Sir Keith Joseph, House of Commons, March
       1985

[16]   Statement by Kenneth Baker, House of Commons, 25 July
       1986

[17]   (Beating bias)
       Peter Newsam
       The Times Educational Supplement, 27 June 1986

[18]   *Draft policy statement on racism*
       ILEA, July 1982

[19]   *Racial attacks*
       Report of a Home Office Study, November 1981

[20]   *Roots*
       Arnold Wesker

[21]   *English from 5 to 16*
       HMI, 1984

[22]   (Reference untraced)
       Alladina

[23]   *The unequal struggle*
       Dr Ashton Gibson, June 1986

[24]   *Curriculum development for a multi-cultural society: policy*
       and curriculum
       Further Education Unit, 1983

[25]   *A language for life*
       Report of the Committee of Inquiry
       (The Bullock Report)
       HMSO, 1975

[26]   Sir Keith Joseph, speech to CLEA, July 1985

[27] Video and manual for GCSE training in English oral assessment.
Secondary Examinations Council, 1986

[28] *Resources for multicultural education: an introduction*
Gillian Klein
Longmans Resource Unit for the Schools Council
Second revised edition 1984

[29] *Reading into racism*
Gillian Klein
Routledge & Kegan Paul, 1985
ISBN 0 7012 0160 5

[30] Evidence submitted by the Schools Council to the Swann Committee

[31] *Curriculum opportunities in a multi-cultural society*
edited by Alma Craft & Geoff Bardell
Harper Education series, 1984

[32] *Agenda for multi-cultural teaching*
Alma Craft & Gillian Klein
SCDC Publications, 1986

[33] *Science education for a multicultural society*
Brian Thompson and a group of Leicestershire teachers
Secondary Science Curriculum Review, 1986

[34] *The seeds of history*
Birley High School, Manchester

[35] *Mathematics Counts*
Report of the Committee of Inquiry into the Teaching of Mathematics in Schools (The Cockroft Report)
HMSO, 1982

[36] *GCSE: The National Criteria*
HMSO, 1985   ISBN 0 11 270569 3

[37] *Black perspectives on FE provision*
Further Education Unit, 1985

[38] *Multi-ethnic education: the way forward*
Alan Little & Richard Willey
Schools Council pamphlet 18, 1981

[39] *Case studies in multi-cultural education*
Ten TV programmes by the Continuing Education

Department, BBC, 1981

[40] *Multi-cultural education: views from the classroom*
John Twitchin & Clare Demuth
BBC, 1981   ISBN 0 563 16443 3

[41] *Education of ethnic minorities*
Schools Council document SC/80/224, 1980

[42] Letter from Peter Dines (deputy chief executive, SEC) to
AMMA, 20 October 1986

[43] *Certificate of pre-vocational education*
Part B: The core competences and vocational module
specifications
Joint Board for Pre-Vocational Education
January 1985

[44] Speech by Frank Cousins to the Annual Conference of the
Institute of Careers Officers, 1969

[45] *Looking for work: black and white school leavers in*
Lewisham
Commission for Racial Equality, 1978

[46] *The education of the black child in Britain: the myth of*
multi-racial education
Maureen Stone
Fontana, 1981

[47] *Minority group experience of the transition from education*
to work
Sheila Allen & Christopher Smith
HMSO, 1975

[48] *Teacher education and training*
Report of the Committee (The James Report)
HMSO, 1972

[49] *Discussion paper on multicultural and antiracist education*
Council for National Academic Awards, 1984

[50] Resolution at AMMA Assembly, Sheffield, 1981

[51] *Increasing the supply of ethnic minority teachers*
DES discussion paper, July 1985

[52] *The collection of ethnically-based statistics on teachers*
and students in teacher training
DES discussion paper, July 1985

[53]   *Positive and negative discrimination in multi-cultural Britain*
       AMMA Conference report, 1983
[54]   Report of the working group on the collection of ethnic
       statistics
       DES, July 1986
[55]   *Code of Practice for the elimination of racial discrimination
       and the promotion of equality of opportunity in
       employment*
       Commission for Racial Equality, July 1983
       ISBN 0 907920 29 2
[56]   *Christmas Broadcast 1982*
       Her Majesty the Queen
[57]   *Education in a multi-ethnic society: an aide-memoire for
       the Inspectorate*
       ILEA Multi-Ethnic Inspectorate Team

Appendix 2

A check-list for schools and colleges

In Chapter 8 we argued that there is a need for institutions to monitor their procedures to see that they are being observed as intended and to assess the extent to which they are fulfilling their aims. This check-list is intended to make some suggestions to schools and colleges about the questions they need to ask themselves about their policies and procedures in the context of the multi-cultural society.

A more detailed check-list with the same purpose can be found in the ILEA Inspectorate document [57].

Questions for heads, principals and senior management teams.

1. What ethnic groups are represented in the school or college (including staff)?
    How has this pattern changed?
    What responses do these changes call for?
    How do we collect and store this information?
    Who has access to it?
2. Are changes needed in our curriculum policy to enhance multi-cultural and anti-racist elements across the whole curriculum?
3. What mother tongues are spoken by our pupils?
    Does our language policy reflect this?
4. Do we have a formal statement of policy defining unacceptable racist activities?
    Are there clear procedures for dealing with them?
    Do they work?
5. How good are we at knowing about the incidence of racial harassment and tension inside and outside the school?
6. What supplementary and community schools exist in the community?

In what ways are they enriching the educational and cultural experience of the school or college community?

7.   What formal and informal contacts do we have with ethnic, religious and cultural groups within the community?

8.   Are the major festivals of all religions represented in the school or college listed on its calendar in the same way as Easter?

What effects will they have on our functions? Do any dates need to be changed?

How do we mark these festivals in the life of the school or college?

9.   Do any of our practices clash with those of any of the ethnic groups in our community?

10. What information is available for staff who may be taking pupils who do not hold British passports on overseas visits? Is up-to-date information on visa requirements available?

Questions for the staff as a whole

1.   How do we respond to linguistic diversity in the classroom? Do pupils for whom English is not their first language (or who speak noticeably non-standard forms of English) receive appropriate ESL support and mother-tongue maintenance?

To what extent do these pupils share the same curricular experiences as others?

2.   Are pupils kept aware of the variety of ethnic groups within the community and appreciative of their different traditions and customs?

3.   Do we know the dietary habits of ethnic groups represented in the school or college and their implications for school meals, end-of-term parties, school visits etc?

4.   Do we know the major religious and other festivals of our pupils and the effects they may have on attendance, extra-curricular activities, sporting fixtures, school functions, parents' evenings etc?

5.   Do we mention and recognise these festivals as naturally as the traditional British ones?

6. Do we routinely and naturally use examples in our teaching from life-styles other than those of the host community?
7. What do we do to inform pupils from other ethnic backgrounds of British customs and traditions with which they may not be familiar?
8. Do any of our pupils have problems arising from familiarity with different number systems and alphabets in other cultures?
9. Have internal and external examination results been reviewed?
   What is their ethnic pattern?
   If there is any ethnic bunching, what have we done to find out the causes?
   How can we remedy it?

Questions for pastoral staff

1. Do we have complete information on the ethnic origin, language and religion of the families of all pupils?
   Is this information available to teachers?
2. Have any racist activities by pupils been noticed?
   If so, what have we done about them?
   Were there any signs we can note to help anticipate such activities in the future?
3. Are any of our pupils the victims of racial harassment?
   Would we know about it if it happened out of school?
4. Which pupils are literate in their mother tongue(s) as well as English?
   Is this bi- or multilingualism given the same esteem as it would be if the other language was French or German?
   Do we have records of pupils' capabilities in different languages?
   Do we mention these capabilities in reports and profiles?
5. What provision is there for pupils to discuss racial and ethnic matters with staff, both formally and informally?
6. Do the records of employment of our leavers include ethnic details?
   What evidence do they give of any racial bias by employers?
   What corrective action can we take?

Questions for governing bodies

1. What are the different ethnic groups represented in the local community and in the school or college?
   How many are represented on the governing body?
   Is this adequate?
2. What contacts do the governors (collectively and individually) have with the different ethnic groups in the community?
   How do we plan to extend this?
3. What statistics on the ethnic composition of the school are available?
4. What ethnic groups are represented on the teaching and support staff and in what numbers?
   Is there any need to take this into consideration in making future appointments?
   How do we advertise posts?
   Are there any ethnic implications in this practice?
   Do we know and use the techniques of bias-free interviewing?
   Should we ask for training in this?
5. Does the school or college have a multi-cultural curriculum policy?
6. Does the school or college have an anti-racist policy and strategies?
   Do we support the staff in implementing these strategies?

Questions for the PTA

1. What activities organised by the PTA have a particular appeal to each ethnic group?
2. Are any ethnic groups represented in the school but conspicuous by their absence from the PTA?
   If so, what can we do about this?
   Is there a need for smaller functions for separate ethnic groups to meet staff and leaders of the PTA?
3. Do any of the school's routines conflict with any minority group customs and practices?
   If so, can we help to resolve the conflict?

Appendix 3

Members of the AMMA Multi-Cultural Education Working Party 1984–86

Dr M L Stevens (Chairman)	Tulse Hill School, Brixton
Mr B Thompson (Vice-Chairman)	St Paul's RC Comprehensive School, Leicester
Mrs L E Brown	St George School, Bristol
Miss E A Gray	Wakefield Girls' High School, Yorkshire
Mr R A Rowe	Shenley Court School, Birmingham
Mrs B Sam-Bailey	St Mark's School, Fulham
Mrs S Whiteley	Rutherford School, Newcastle upon Tyne

The working party has also had the help of a number of corresponding members who have read and advised on draft material. These members have extended the range of expertise on which the group could draw to include the primary sector, a teachers' centre and several parts of the country and ethnic groups not represented on the main group.

Appendix 4

A pre-publication seminar

On 3 March, the Assistant Masters and Mistresses Association held a seminar to discuss the themes developed in this book. Those who attended each had a copy of the text of "Multi-Cultural and Anti-racist Education Today." This appendix is a verbatim transcript of what participants said.

(Mrs. Cynthia Watmore in the Chair)

THE CHAIRMAN: I begin with a welcome from AMMA and headquarters. I am delighted, as the Vice-President of the Association, to welcome you and to have the opportunity to say how much the Association appreciates the work that Dr. Mike Stevens and his working party do in developing our thinking on multi-cultural education – and, of course, the update that we are here to discuss today.

That update is the result of a great deal of hard work and hours of discussion. I am sure that there are many points that we shall develop today.

First of all I call on Dr. Mike Stevens to open the debate.

DR. M. L. STEVENS (Chairman, Working Party): It is a great pleasure to welcome here today a group of colleagues with varying kinds of involvement in multi-cultural and anti-racist education who have responded to our invitation to join us at the last stage of preparing our new publication. You have all had the opportunity to read the text of our new policy statement, which has already been approved by the Executive Committee. Our purpose today is an exchange of professional views which will be noted and appended to the document when it is published.

It is nearly four years since we published our last policy booklet on this subject and a great deal has happened in that time – not least the Swann report and the various responses to it. Indeed, the idea of our new publication was originally for a response to Swann, but when we started planning it we realised that so much debate was going on in different places that we needed a much more comprehensive look at the whole subject area.

We saw a need to do two things. Our own members needed to be informed and updated on the continuing public debate in the whole area, and we also felt that we should bring together and publish all the various ideas on the subject, which we as an Association have developed over the last four years through our participation in conferences, responding to documents, and all the other things that have gone on.

Some of the chapters in the new booklet needed only very slight updating from the old one. In the area of the curriculum, for example, we were able to note an increased awareness of the concept of a multi-cultural curriculum, although the rationalisation of the necessity has not yet been followed in all cases by the consummation of the reality. In examinations, the arrival of GCSE and CPVE have produced opportunities for major changes. Moves in the direction of limiting bias in examining have been accompanied by some worthy statements of intent in that direction from the Schools Examination Council and various other authorities. We shall keep a watch over the next few years on how well those intentions are turned into established practices.

In other areas, particularly that of language, our thinking has undergone a more drastic development. In the period since our last publication, there has been a great deal of public debate about language in education, not only in the multi-cultural context, but elsewhere as well. This has produced a number of new insights which we see as potentially helpful for students for whom English is not the first language.

We originally voiced two principles in this area. On the one hand, we clearly believe that such children should be helped to mastery of all the different registers of English that they will need in their everyday life. On the other hand, they need to be educated in a context that acknowledges, respects and

133

sustains the language – or, often, the languages – of their homes. Alongside that original twofold concern, we now place a new emphasis on working methods that will enable such students to share as much as possible of the curriculum and the activities on offer to their contemporaries: hence a new emphasis on main-class support, as opposed to withdrawing those students and teaching them separately.

The whole question of ethnic monitoring in education and employment has become much more prominent in the public debate in the last three years. AMMA has involved itself, nationally and locally in many parts of the country, in discussions and negotiations on this subject. The document before you collates our views on both the principles and the practices of such monitoring exercises.

But the biggest change that has come over the debate in recent years has been in what has been said about racism in education. The Rampton report brought to public view much that had been below the surface for a long time. In 1983, when we published the previous document, I would have been surprised if our Executive Committee had approved a document with the word "anti-racist" in the title. The phrase then was seen too much as the property of those who produced resounding slogans with little intellectual backing. Such people still exist, but now no document about multi-cultural education could be convincing without directly facing the issue of racism. I hope that we have done this in the new document. We have tried to look behind the slogans to seek the underlying issues that need to be addressed and to offer our contribution to addressing them.

It has been most unfortunate that multi-cultural and anti-racist aspects of education have been seen by so many people as in opposition to each other. In our view, they are absolutely complementary. Neither can succeed without the other. We see one overriding concern. Our objective is a society that not only tolerates but enjoys diversity. To this end, we think it proper for people from minority groups to be in a position to make their own choice of the extent to which their lifestyles draw on their ancestral culture and other cultures in whose midst they live.

If that choice is to be an informed one, multi-cultural education has an important role to play. The widespread existence of racist attitudes and practices on the part of members of the indigenous majority cannot be denied. We need immediately effective short-term programmes of action to defend people against those attitudes and practices. But once again, only a genuinely multi-cultural education for all can deliver the long-term changes in attitude that will diminish and eventually remove the need for the immediate measures. In this respect, it is the "White Highlands" where the need is greatest.

As we say in our final chapter:

"Without immediate anti-racist strategies, ethnic minorities will not be able to take the first steps in overcoming the obstacles created by prejudice, and the long-term aims of a multi-cultural curriculum will not be achievable. Without a multi-cultural curriculum to lay an improved foundation of thought for future generations, anti-racism will never have the chance to be more than a form of crisis-management."

MR. HARLEY STRATTON (St. Mary's College): On a point of procedure. Do you intend to go through the booklet chapter by chapter?

DR. STEVENS: I had not thought of any particular structure; I like to keep these discussions free-form. If you have any particular comments, we should like to hear them.

MR. STRATTON: I think just general questions first; there are specific things that I want to ask later.

MISS ANN GRAY (Working Party): It might be helpful at this stage to say that we were particularly responsible for thinking out, and leading thinking on, the language section – not only in chapter 3 but wherever it might impinge on the other sections. I think that it was here that we became aware quite quickly that, having studied Swann carefully, but also having moved ourselves because of influences at about that time, we had not only to decide whether we were going to shift our ground and suggest such a shift in the official document of the Association: we were also beginning to feel, I think, that the movement of thought towards any position that we might feel was the right one should be fully spelled out in the chapter. That is why we wanted to write it in the way we did.

I was very aware, from looking at the older booklet, that the emphasis there was getting very dated – it was speaking a great deal about new arrivals and so on. I was very aware, for other reasons as well, of what we mention here – the two sorts of voice speaking to us, taking opposing views and making very powerful advocacy a great deal of the time of two different approaches.

It was about the time when I was seeing Laurie Fallows' work at the end of the days of the Schools Council, and more than once, we corresponded or spoke on the telephone. I was interested, from the English Committee of the Schools Council, in what he was saying, because I was working on the criteria for GCSE. He, at the same time, was monitoring and thinking out his recommendations about language and literature from the multi-cultural point of view. I think there were times when I was very much exercised to sort out my views and then could not always agree with him, but it was interesting for us to compare our attitudes.

On the one hand, at just about that time, I was hearing a great deal about the greater desire for recognition of the expression that was natural to children in their own homes and their own families. Particularly Harold Rosen was speaking about this in a general way, and we were also hearing about it from some of the West Indian community particularly.

On the other hand, we were getting very loud representations and very angry calls to narrow our teaching of English in general in schools, to get down to the things that were going to be of practical importance to those who were going to have to face interviews where people would be unfair to them and so on, where people would latch on to any way of criticising their presentation in order to deny them the opportunities of jobs.

In order to think about those two opposing ways of seeing the situation, we tried to present first of all our recognition of the concern and the sincerity of both camps. Then, we had to say what we were going to do about that when we are in the classroom, having to think as teachers about what we are going to do. In the end, I felt that we had to come back to those two principles that Mike said we had studied earlier, but which became far more meaningful to us as we faced this sort of controversy.

In the first place, I think that there was no way in which we could ignore the needs of those children who would be required on certain occasions to use standard English as it is generally recognised, but we could not agree that we should be teaching that to any children – whether they were the West Indian children or people in my own home district of Barnsley and Doncaster – unless it was part of the idea of repertoire in the school. I could not agree with the view that some of those parents were expressing and that Laurie Fallows came to express in one or two of his pieces of writing – that we were so anxious about their language needs in that direction that we would willingly narrow down those children's exposure to a wide range of literature which was similar to the sort of literature and experience that we would give in the widest and richest English lessons to all children.

I kept worrying about the children in Leeds or Barnsley, for example, who might be given a narrower range of literature constantly. I wondered when on earth they would graduate from that narrower experience, very much concentrating on their own environment, and move out and become part of a wider community.

So in some way, we were trying, as we were writing that chapter, to reconcile those two needs. We really need your guidance as to how we have done it – whether we have done it in a reasonable way and whether our thinking is making sense to people who have come to us.

MRS. LILIAN BROWN (Working Party): My school is on the edge of St. Paul's and many of our pupils come from St. Paul's. One thing that the chapter on language throws up very forcibly is the problems for the English teacher, and especially for teachers such as myself, who are somewhat long in the tooth, and who have not been given any training in the skills which are mentioned in that chapter. Those are the skills of accepting the register of West Indian children, so that they can take a pride in their own language. The suggestion is that this needs some specialised training, especially in English departments, where there are not language specialists. In my own school, this was increasingly the case, as there was a cut in staffing. This is a very valid point which needs a good airing, because the resources are not available in the schools, and I think they need to be.

MR. STRATTON: I am slightly confused because of the chronology of events which surround this matter. Specialists are emerging from places such as where I work, from teacher training colleges and so on. There are specialists in E2L and in general multi-lingual concerns. These people have been trained. They have done postgraduate courses or initial training, and they will have done a B.Ed., which has a low input in respect of this particular specialism. So there are waves of people going out into the schools who are highly qualified and specialist in this one area. But events have overtaken them and we have a totally different set-up. There is now a clash between the reception situations in many schools in London, for example, and language centres, for example, which have not been entirely phased out – let us be honest about it, they are still around.

So children are being withdrawn for specialist language help and are receiving it from the teachers. On the other hand, the classroom teacher is grappling with the very real problems of the E2L learner and others as well. He is not sure what to do. So support teams are drawn in from the old system, which is the language centre, and there is a general confusion of services. I was unsure about this myself, because I am supposed to be training people to do that in one area or the other, and I am not sure whether I can do both. This is a problem for me, and I should welcome some comments from people in the field.

MISS GRAY: We are very aware that this whole situation was still too riddled with the negative stereotypes that we were warned about and which we actually acknowledged in the report. But the point that Harley Stratton has made is certainly an important one, about the support teams – that a number of different specialisms were beginning to be imported, but the way in which they worked was not brought out.

MRS. SHEENA S. WHITELEY (Working Party): It is really necessary to have E2L people who are language experts. I have had discussions about this with section 11 people, who appear to feel, certainly locally, that English is not the number one thing, that the section 11 approach is just introducing it to the school curriculum; and because there is a shortage of people with this expertise, people are being appointed who do not have it. That may be solved over time, but it is essential to have all teachers trained with some sort of E2L input. I have asked postgraduate students who have come to us about this and I find that it has very little, if anything at all, to do with multi-cultural education. It is very sad.

I am very concerned about point (iii) on page 24; "Yet others speak English as their first language, but with pronunciation, grammatical structures, vocabulary and speech rhythms which diverge sharply from what, with all its variations, is called 'Standard English'."

As many of the children are in inner-city schools, they are perhaps picking up the language of their peers, which is only natural.

You might think that I came from an area where Geordie itself might be regarded as E2L; but this problem can lead to great misunderstandings, particularly in the business of speech rhythms, the way in which words are pronounced. We listen to tones in English, and if people speak with a different intonation, it can give a different impression. For instance, if you go to the bank and say, "This is the *wrong* form," the person to whom you are speaking interprets that as rather rude or abrupt, when it may not be meant like that. This really is very important.

So we could do with many more English teachers. Schools need more English staff. Also – this is a point brought out in other chapters – with GCSE, many staff in other departments have to do oral assessments and there is no training in this for them at all. On the oral side, therefore, we need more resources and more staff.

MS. GILLIAN KLEIN (Multi-Cultural Teaching): If we are going to talk about teacher training, I should like to see the debate widened outside language. I am willing to stop there if you want to come back to the language questions, and raise the issue again. I know about the MA at St. Mary's College, but what happens with the general students who come in? I am running a DES 1/86 course at Warwick University for teachers; there is an MA there in multi-cultural education. Professor John Eggleston obviously leads the field there, and his students and tutor group are getting it, but what is the permeation into the B.Ed. there? This debate has to be taken widely. It should not be only English issues; it should be broadened to include pedagogy and the ethos of the school. I should like to see it debated along that paradigm.

MRS. BROWN: We take that up, don't we, in what we say about teacher training and the diversity of colleges and universities?

MS. LEMAH BONNICK (Institute of Education): I too should like to see the debate widened beyond the question of language itself. I often feel concerned that, when the issue of language – be it English as a second language or direct speakers – is discussed, we tend to isolate the teaching of English in junior schools from dominant trends within English teaching over the last couple of years. The more dominant tendency of English teachers has been to teach English as a subject dealing with issues rather than as a subject dealing with the techniques, the mechanisms, the structure of the language.

I would want researchers and teachers to address themselves to the implication of the former focus of English teaching for children – dialect speakers and other minorities – for whom English is not their first language. Perhaps we have to question whether we should shift the emphasis – not just to think of the teaching of the English as something that these children need but actually to look at what sort of mechanisms there have been in schools over the last 20 years and relate their acquisition of English to dominant practices in the schools.

MISS GRAY: We are now touching on one of the great dilemmas in English teaching and teaching in general in schools. I am sure that Ms. Bonnick is right to say that much of our teaching was moving away to concentrate on issues and topics and so on. Many teachers were not really learning how to speak about and help the children with some understanding of the mechanisms and techniques of oral and written language and expression. On the other hand, we are now swinging between two extremes in a very unhappy way. Ms. Bonnick was speaking about a confusion among all English teachers – or at any rate, many of them – which must be sorted out. They either do one or the other, and they do not know how to marry the two, or to do either properly.

MS. BONNICK: My problem is that, if one addresses the problems of English acquisitions by non-indigenous children without addressing them within the framework of dominant school practice, one tends to focus their needs as if somehow they are outside the frame of reference of other children. I have taught in school and I know that some of the mistakes that English children make in respect of verbs and so on are very common. Yet the case is often made as if those problems are unique to ethnic minority children.

MISS GRAY: That brings me back to the point, that the greater insight that we need into the techniques of teaching is for all children, and that we should not swing from the topics or the issues to a very narrow set of special guidance and so on. There has to be something which marries the two.

MRS. MARGARET PROCTER (Association of Career Teachers): Is this not a case for more collaborative teaching, of putting the support teachers into the classroom – the experts, or so-called experts, on the language side? I am talking mainly from a primary point of view, but I can see it working in secondary schools too – there the support teacher goes in and works alongside the class teacher, perhaps taking the main part of the lesson, emphasising the language side of the lesson, irrespective of what subject you are covering.

DR. STEVENS: When we are talking about the needs of children for whom English is not the first language, how you can do it in the school rather depends on the resourcing available and the numbers of children who need that kind of help. If a school has a fairly small number of E2L students and therefore fairly limited resources to offer them, to use that resourcing in the form of main-class support may be spreading it too thinly. I suspect that, the higher the proportion of E2L students in a school, the easier it is to marshal your resources in that way. Educationally, it is the best way to deliver this support if you can, but it is not always possible.

MRS. WHITELEY: There are practical difficulties about this as well. It can cause resentment in a community where all the children need some linguistic help – the kind of children referred to in paragraph 36 of the draft report about dialect speakers. There are many practical difficulties about this. For example, on page 42, we way:

> "How can teachers co-ordinate the practical arrangements within the classroom for the successful implementation of support teaching?"

One thing that we asked for here was flexibility, because the ideal has not been realised. Different schools are at different stages. If people forge ahead saying that this is what must be done, without taking account of local circumstances, everybody will lose out.

MRS. BROWN: I come back to Ms. Klein's point about opening up the whole discussion on training. In our chapter on teachers and teacher education, we comment on a paper included in the Swann report about the diversity of teacher training to be found in the polytechnics and universities. Recently – last July – with the new validations and so forth, I went to the University of Bristol to see the new training schemes for teachers and how the schools have co-ordinated. I talked about the multi-cultural content of training. It amounted, even in this day and age, to one half day. When I protested about this, the justification was: "There are so many things that students have to deal with today".

Going back to the "White Highlands" that Dr. Stevens mentioned, and the areas where there is very little appreciation of the multi-cultural content of the curriculum, how are we going to tally the issue of anti-racism with Dr. Stevens's statement that society not only tolerates but enjoys diversity, when the local authorities themselves are not making much provision for INSET on multi-cultural aspects, never mind what is coming in in the new teaching course?

MR. BRIAN THOMPSON (Working Party): We have heard how this affects teachers of all subjects. In the new examinations, when a specific assessment has to be made and recorded for reporting and recording results, which can be in writing or spoken, the teacher finds that a candidate or a student – it is difficult to distinguish between the two when they are going to be entered for an examination and you are assessing them from week one – reports the science area correctly, but in the kind of speech that you would have found difficulty with in a normal situation. You come up against the fact that this is good communication, despite that. They have got the message.

When the actual need for clarity in reporting was not defined, and it was left to the teachers' own whim, one occasionally forgot that one was trying to see how good a student was at reporting on one's subject, and not how nicely he spoke. I speak as one who was turned down for a job in Willenhall on the basis that Geordie was not acceptable. I would love to say that the headmaster was a Scot, but he was not: he was Welsh.

143

MR. PETER SMITH (Deputy General Secretary): Mr. Manyan was telling me before the meeting that he was a professional linguist who teaches languages. I should be interested in his views of these issues as they strike a professional teacher of languages.

MR. WINSTON MANYAN (Caribbean Teachers' Association): In our department, we are the only ones who attend to the issues of mechanisms – that is, grammar. We seem to be the outcasts, and I suppose that that goes for others.

My view also is that this approach is necessary. I think that it was removed from examination syllabuses as early as 1962 or 1963 – 25 years ago – when I remember specifically that analysis was on the O-level examination paper. Current ideas such as GCSE have condoned this practice in schools, because they have not really emphasised this approach to any extent. I suspect that it will be required to get the grades A, B or C, and the others will just have to sink. That is how I look at it. Some teachers in the department are torn over how to structure their teaching for the new exam which started in September. This is the dilemma in the languages department.

MRS. WHITELEY: This is very common with teacher course work – not the course, but there is not the time.

MS. GENE SNELLGROVE (Working Party): I start at the bottom end of the age scale. I have nursery children. There are local indigenous white children who come to school not speaking terribly good English, but the Caribbean children are always far more articulate and clear. Their sentence construction is better. I have had only one Caribbean child go for speech therapy.

As for the Indian children, if they come to school not speaking English, they do not speak it at all. This is an area where the majority of children speak English, not somewhere like Southall, where the majority speak Hindustani or other languages of the Indian sub-continent. They may not speak for two or three terms. If they are busy and they play and do things for themselves, it is all right. The only children that we have to worry about are those who do not know how to play – they are handicapped. But at the end of that time, suddenly, the English comes out in chunks; properly constructed. It is as if they have built it up inside themselves until they have the confidence to bring it out.

MRS. B. SAM-BAILEY (Working Party): In the Caribbean, all the children are taught grammar at an early age. As part of the curriculum, we have to do analysis and parsing, looking at the structure of the sentence and analysing it according to the parts of speech. This is why you find that the children can speak grammatically. When we arrive here, we might not have the same accent, but it is noticeable in England that people from different parts of the country have their own identities and accents. Therefore, we bring our own into Britain – but that does not mean that we do not understand English or do not speak it grammatically.

MISS GRAY: It is interesting just at the moment that there is a tremendous thrust in proposals for teaching courses in linguistics, and establishing A-level courses in the study of linguistics of the English language. It is not something difficult but is done at the lower levels in the school. Also of course, there are warring camps about the linguistic experts, so one has to ally oneself with one school or another before one gets going.

MR. J. S. BEASTALL (Department of Education and Science): I find this very interesting and educative. In looking at the question of English as a second language these days, HMI feels that the technique of in-class support is superior to the withdrawal to separate units and so on. I can quite understand that it is much easier where there is a high proportion of ethnic minority pupils than where you have only a few. In terms of how one goes in the future, of course, this is not something which can ever be enforced by a diktat, but it would be helpful if we were all marching in the same direction on this, because of the problem of training and so on. Having listened to the arguments, it seems to me that that could be our objective – to revive this primary method of help by having support teachers in the classroom.

One point which arose earlier on was the question of section 11 teachers. We are very anxious, apart from achieving the best use of grant money, that such teachers should have clear job descriptions. This is happening in some authorities, and we are trying to encourage it in all of them, but some certainly have a good way to go on this. It is absolutely crucial that section 11 teachers should have it spelled out in black and white what is their task – whether to offer support in the classroom or in some other way. Perhaps the Association can do its bit in demanding job descriptions in those circumstances.

Training to me, coming from the centre, has to be the most important aspect of this. As you no doubt know, we have made multi-cultural aspects of teaching and the curriculum one of the national priorities in the latest INSET system. Again, it is very important that authorities are encouraged to make full use of this. Some are better than others at doing so. In particular, some of the shire counties are slow in taking up all these opportunities. Again, any influences that can be brought to bear on the actual practitioners would be very useful.

THE CHAIRMAN: One of the difficulties with some of the local authorities in the shire areas in particular is finding the correct provider for such courses. One can set up all kinds of in-service training and have all kinds of priorities, but if you do not have the people to give the instruction and to lead the groups who are there waiting for the information and the new techniques and the background it is almost an impossible task. It comes back to the whole area of training and also to the section 11 arrangements.

Those teachers, as support teachers, will in their way require training as well. The difficulties seem to be in that area, of finding places where teachers may be trained or re-trained to do the support teaching as well as main stream teaching. That is something that we might be able to emphasise still further with the Department, through our membership, to the local authorities which are going out and putting in the bids and finding the providers with the expertise to do this job.

MR. BEASTALL: That is the point of what I was saying. There may be scope for co-operation between authorities on a regional basis.

MRS. WHITELEY: There is something which could be done by teachers themselves. I stood up and said this at a great big meeting in Newcastle, but the minute I mentioned money, everybody went terribly quiet. I suggested that they put their money where their mouth was. Why do they not close the schools for half a day, so that all teachers could get together? There is a great danger that one or perhaps two staff are designated "the multi-cultural teachers" and they are sent off: "That is his pigeon, her pigeon." In a school with perhaps 100 staff, there will be all kinds of opinions. The only way is to have a day set aside. We found it valuable to have such an exercise to discuss the GCSE, for instance. Similarly, let us have half a day when all the staff were called together and we had working groups on this subject. We could divide up and there would be a time to discuss, a time to disagree, a time at where it was possible to disagree and discuss.

There is sometimes a great danger that it is not possible to disagree on these matters. If you are working with staff, you know one or two people on the staff whose attitude is quite unhealthy. I have on occasion challenged at least a couple of members for comments that they have made – to their surprise. Teachers could do that. It is no good just thinking of INSET as something which will come from without. It could start from within and perhaps that would throw up the necessary comments or suggestions from the staff themselves.

MR. BEASTALL: In the long run, it is all down to initial teacher training. It is important to get the right attitude, to get across the concept that this is not one little extra bit but a fundamental part of the whole teaching job. In due course, when the message finally gets through to the teacher training institutions, in practice rather than in theory – we have a theory at the moment, but the practice remains to be seen – I hope that that will meet the point. Therefore, it will be the natural thing for all staff in the school to be taught about this as they are taught about all other aspects of their task. In the shorter run, we have a very large INSET job to do. That is why it is a national priority.

MR. MANYAN: Following from this suggestion of a full day or half a day for a conference, I should like to see coming from that the creation of a course departmental group, an ongoing committee, which would represent the whole school and move forward with a policy – agency in-service training.

MRS. WHITELEY: Having had experience, I know that it is very easy to have a cosmetic committee. I resigned from just such a committee because I asked awkward questions and at the end of the year I was the only member of staff who turned up to see how things were going. It needs a push and people should not wait to speak. They should get up and speak when they are genuinely interested. It does not matter what their scale is; they are all equal on the committee. People should listen to one another and get going.

MR. MANYAN: As for the point of the committee being cosmetic, it would be better if we made it a genuine committee. I am very chary of these "big bang" half-day conferences, where everyone speaks and nothing flows from it. There should be a purpose in view.

THE CHAIRMAN: It it is part of the school curriculum policy and the school in-service policy, a school-focused in-service policy, with cross-curricular activity, and if it could be inserted somewhere in the local authority policy and the school policy, it would have its place in discussion across the whole area of the curriculum. Just as music and aesthetic appreciation are part of an entitlement curriculum at the moment, perhaps this is another area where we could be looking and developing further. This is another projection really for LEAs and schools to take up.

MS. KLEIN: Cost is hardly a factor in training, I think. Taking HMI's point, it is part of professionalism. It should be taught from the beginning of teacher training in every institution which is in any way accrediting teachers. Then I hope that in all the professional bodies – this is where AMMA has a vital role to play – it will be seen as part of professionalism, part of good practice and a sound understanding of the issues around us, and a response to societal change in education – the fact that we need different kinds of education for different reasons; technology is another. As long as this permeates, it will be one of the principal ways, but you will need some kind of impetus.

Trouble arises in areas where there is low ethnic minority settlement, where you will get the attitude: "We do not have a problem here." Then the pressures have to come from outside. It has to be made clear that we are talking just as much about the education of white children in our cultural plurality and our divided and unequal society. That conflation of education in a just multi-cultural society is talking about what we would like to happen, not what is happening – and we have to be clear on that. There has to be a continued pressure, direction, leadership, from professional bodies, LEAs and so on.

But when it comes to actually doing it, there are two main things to bear in mind. First of all, I would argue that the expertise is here in terms of people whose legs carry them around the country as fast as they can. It is extraordinary to see this travelling show of genuine expertise, with people learning as they go along. If one listens to Ranjit Arora, who spoke on my course yesterday, one will note that she is not saying what she said three years ago. She is saying new things. People are learning from each other, and the expertise is there. It is also documented. The literature is vast these days and it is well worth reading. You can give an impetus by inspiration. I very much take the point that the "big bang" of half a day is not enough, but it is sometimes a good stimulus.

But the point is the follow-up, which must come from the LEA and the individual school. I am a believer in school-based work. I know one school in ILEA which is doing it right through the year. There can be paranoia about working parties being responsible for multi-cultural education, and there can be pigeon-holing when the job is given to one person. It has to be shared, but it must be monitored. Michael Marlan has given a good model of how this monitoring has to take place. Teachers have to evaluate their work and in so doing must monitor anti-racist multi-cultural education all the time.

In that way, we would get some kind of cascade effect. That technique is the way of getting the expertise to permeate, to get itself to all members of schools and staffs. That seems to me to be a very valuable thing.

These DES 1/86 courses, like the one that I am running at Warwick, are looking at ways of supporting teachers and continuing the work when they get back into their authorities. I have chosen those words carefully I am not saying "into their schools" only – certainly there, but in their authorities as well, which will have an educative role afterwards.

These are some of the techniques that I have observed going on in the country for some time.

MISS GRAY: As people have been speaking, I have been thinking of two points. First of all, I have thought for a long time, and I know that colleagues have thought, that in general, teachers – for their own good in the future – needed to show themselves more ready to act as well-informed professionals and to acquaint themselves with the important documents which were crucial to debates of this kind. Therefore, that kind of cynicism about some of the documents which are important and which should inform the debate has to be broken down.

On the other hand, there is another aspect. Sometimes, although the expert and the researcher must support all this, nevertheless, very often, our members – the ordinary teachers showing an everyday interest – can show that what has seemed to other people an alien element – the work of the expert out there – has some relevance to something which has just happened in the last lesson in the school. That is what will have an impact on those who are antagonistic. Therefore, among our members, we must reinterpret some of this and show them the relevance of it. That is the role that we must play and that we can go on playing when this document has come out.

150

My second point relates to what many of us remember from last summer in our schools. Mine is a school where it is not very easy to get department meetings very often, but when we had our day and we closed, people in the departments all over the place sat down and talked in the most productive way. Everybody looked back and said, "We have to do it in that way." It was not a "big bang" day; it was doing what we always knew we had to do, and we were working through things in a much more sensible way than we had ever managed before.

We must feed that ingredient into that sort of discussion, which I think will happen in many schools. Many of them are planning through this year days when we are not importing experts but when we are all sitting down in departments and thinking through what has happened to us over GCSE this year. That is the opportunity for some of this to be fed in again, in the immediate future anyway.

MS. BONNICK: I am very sympathetic to that, and I do not want to be too cynical, but I have just completed research on how further education colleges in Inner London have received the ILEA directives on anti-racism and sexism and whatever. I know that many teachers do feel put upon. They feel that they have not been taught how to make their subject areas multi-cultural and responsive to the needs of various minorities. They feel that this is a case of someone else asking them to take on more than they can cope with. It is probably to do with us not being able to define clearly what the objectives are and what areas are going to be renegotiated in the schools.

In a curious way, when we talk of multi-culturalism and multi-ethnicism, the white groups have defined themselves out of that area, and in an unconscious way, teachers have done the same. They do not see it as something which involves everybody. Their conceptual structures cannot deal with this, so the teachers feel that it is something for the minorities, and perhaps they are focusing too much attention on the ethnic minorities because they are not part of that group and they have defined themselves out of ethnicity. Therefore, they see it as something to do with these other groups of children that we are always talking about and giving attention to.

I do not know how one gets away from it and how we start renegotiating the whole area of the curriculum. Somebody talked about linguistics bringing in new conceptual structures, so that we can achieve a fusion, and normalise that fusion; at the moment, it is abnormal to too many people – even well-intentioned people who are trying to get it off the ground.

MS. KLEIN: ILEA is a special case, because there is at the moment immense anxiety among white teachers, who recognise, perhaps correctly, that they should not be defining what should go into this response: it is not for them to tell people what is good for them, especially on the basis of ethnicity; it is highly inappropriate. That has caused some stepping back and some anxiety, if not panic, among some white people. The leadership needs to come from elsewhere on that.

The point of linguistics or language awareness programmes or that kind of extension of the curriculum to a wider framework overall must be the appropriate response. That comes back to a general evaluation of good practice, but it means that we have to be teaching different things.

MS. BONNICK: And broadening the conceptual areas of our own subject areas and normalising that process. I feel profoundly that many teachers believe that the broadening is not quite normal, that talking about something other than English literature in an English literature lesson is not normal: "You cannot be doing American literature in this area; there is something wrong with this." Their own insecurity is somehow transmitted to their pupils, who feel that this is marginal. The pedagogy, because it is uncertain, is transmitted in an uncertain way, and they do not actually deliver what it is we hoped they would.

MS. KLEIN: It is a new language. That is why so much of my work is in the curriculum area, and part of the agenda for multi-cultural teaching looks at the curriculum. There was a piece recently in "Science" which pointed out that the

152

so-called "Halley's comet" had been known in the East for centuries before anyone had heard of Halley. Science has to learn new things and that is true in all curricular areas. It is scary and threatening, when you have been teaching the same thing for 15 years, to realise that you must teach something new. That is where we must address initial teacher training – to ensure that people learn a different approach to their pedagogy and that they increase their own areas of knowledge, right through their teaching careers.

DR. STEVENS: I should like to pick up Lemah Bonnick's point about how FE teachers feel put upon because they have not been taught to do this. That is true, but in itself it is a faint-hearted approach. Much multi-cultural development has come from teachers in the classroom in schools such as mine. Fifteen years ago, English, history and RE teachers in my school started developing their own materials long before the ILEA World History Project got off the ground.

Teachers are actually pretty resourceful people. They can get on and start developing materials. Schools that are starting now, as Gillian said – due in no small part to her own efforts in this field – find lots of stuff available to help them. They are not doing it all from scratch, as my colleagues were 15 years ago; there is a lot going on. There are now more appropriate exam syllabuses available if you look for them. That was the big fight waged by our history people – getting exam boards to accept world history ideas as valid for an examinable course. It was an immense struggle, but that struggle has been won and it is easier for people starting now. The big problem is getting teachers aware of the need, particularly in white suburbia.

It is the suburban areas which are the most worrying. There are relatively few areas left which are all-white, but those that are, are nearly all in the suburbs. This is where so many schools are ignoring the questions of the multi-cultural nature of society. These of course are the very children who will not necessarily be working in their white suburban areas but in the urban areas down the road, with a racially mixed population

153

for which they have not been prepared. This is the great danger area.

MRS. BROWN: Mike has pre-empted something of what I wanted to say. The whole situation is a pyramid. All pyramids have a firm base, and the base in this case is the classroom teacher. Before I joined the Working Party, I had never heard of Gillian Klein. As you said, Chairman, we are going to need the people to get courses going, to support them and to support the classroom teacher – but how does that tally with where Mrs. Klein started? Did she start from a primary individual enthusiasm? I have been 29 years in my school, which has seen many revolutions. When I started, there were only one or two ethnic pupils. To our shame, one Asian girl in the school was called "Bee-bee". We discovered later that that just meant "girl", so we had been addressing her as "Girl", because that was how her father had registered her. We now have an ethnic population of 20 to 25 per cent. This tallies with Mrs. Klein and people like her – the real nub is the classroom teachers getting off their butts and doing something about it.

MS. KLEIN: That is why I am trying to pass on the information. Mike makes the point that we start from an awareness in Tulse Hill, and the materials produced there are published nationally. That is what I have always been able to pick up. I see my role purely as an information agent in this field.

One thing which has not yet been raised is relevant. In Cornwall, at the end of January, I saw only pink faces. Nobody had any direct experience of visible minorities. But they sure as blazes knew about racism. The reason was quite clear: there is an active National Front and British Movement in Cornwall. I am afraid that there is a declared policy now of recruitment in the "White Highlands". There is another way in, I am afraid – a negative way. This is not the base of the pyramid, of teachers who have considered the issues positively; it is teachers who are recognising now that something needs to be done, and fast.

MR. MANYAN: To continue where I left off, with those graduates from white schools who would be working in a multi-cultural society, and many of whom will assume top jobs in executive positions in senior and middle management, basically, this will perpetuate the practices which are at variance with those in the multi-cultural society. How do you break that spiral?

DR. STEVENS: This is where the prejudice in employment, which we talk about in our chapter on careers, is reinforced all the time.

MR. MANYAN: I think that the draft report is a comprehensive and coherent one. I should like to step ahead and ask how you propose to disseminate the information around your membership. Am I right in saying that the draft was made exclusively for AMMA members? How will the practices impact on the schools?

THE CHAIRMAN: I call on our Deputy General Secretary to answer that.

MR. SMITH: We have not made the final decision about that at the moment. Certainly, the primary purpose of the working party – it has been in existence for some time – was to produce guidance for our own members. If the booklet has a value for teachers and those concerned with multi-cultural and anti-racist education more generally – and obviously, we hope that it has – we would want to make it available.

Our practice usually in these matters – I have to be careful about this, with Harley Stratton here – is to make certain that all the schools in which we have members – there are now 18,000 of them – automatically get a copy of everything we publish, free. We also – this is where I am picking up Harley Stratton – send copies of our literature free on request to colleges of education, the Institute of Education, for example.

Clearly, there is a point beyond which commerce overcomes philanthropy, when you just cannot afford to do it any more on any scale. Therefore, we are contemplating putting a cover price on this booklet. If requests come from the education service, we are not going to say, on the one hand, "We are under-funded," and on the other, "We will contribute to the under-funding."

DR. STEVENS: And of course, we shall be seeking publicity for it. We shall have a press conference for the launch.

MR. THOMPSON: If we follow the example of the one that is now out of print, the first edition did not get much beyond AMMA members and Rampton. The second edition was available in all the university and training establishments in my branch – and not through any effort of mine. It had got there and was found to be valuable. It was available also in the multi-cultural resource centre in the authority. I assume that that sort of thing has been happening in other branches too.

MISS GRAY: We found that we were overwhelmed with requests.

MR. SMITH: I am pursuing Winston's point in a slightly different way. I think that we are all conscious that if you set up any kind of working party which is in itself a creature of an organisation, it is easy for a kind of incestuousness to creep into the thinking. In a sense, however, the question is, what have we got wrong? Where are the gaps? Where is the emphasis wrong? Where are the places which might lead your own organisations to say, "These are intensely well-meaning people, obviously wanting to go in the right direction. What a pity that on that issue they shunted into a siding."

MR. MANYAN: Having read the booklet, we did not find that. We found that it could be used in tandem with a number of other pronouncements. What we pondered on was just how many community workers and so on will take on board the issues raised and the approaches recommended. That is why my question is, how will you disseminate this information now beyond your membership? Schools and head teachers should have copies and knowledge of this booklet. Make no mistake about it – for me, this is a "miniature Swann," and not every school has a Swann report.

MR. SMITH: That is a far more courteous reply than I expected. I am sure that there are people who could be more acerbic.

MISS GRAY: I think that this gives me an opportunity to mention a point which is very important to me. First of all, I do not think that any of us here would wish to speak in whispers about our concern about the multi-cultural issues. We have been working very hard to educate our own members, and we know that there is a substantial job still to do – I would not be quiet about that – among our own membership. We know that. There is an ignorance – sometimes aware, sometimes unaware – about the issues we think are important.

We all know that some of those areas still exist, where there is either complete blankness among AMMA membership sometimes, or in the country at large, or else there is opposition – not of the National Front kind but of the conservative kind, of a different sort. Sometimes, the only way in which we can penetrate those areas is in making those people realise that they are meeting us for other reasons. If we espouse these points and these causes, they do not expect us to be the most militant and active in every way all the time. We have a role. We can penetrate some of these areas among colleagues and people outside our own organisation in schools which other people cannot so easily reach, perhaps.

I am aware, for example, that, not far from my own district, in schools simlar to mine, one saw the entrenched idea of "colour-blindness." Some years ago, in my own school, many people would have thought that that was the best possible attitude to take. Because some very wise people have been working quietly in my school for a long time, that attitude is not likely to be found very much now, and the whole situation has grown and changed in my school.

However, we had to tackle very early on something which did not seem to those people to be anything to do with what is in this booklet. We had to insist over and over again in all our general studies work that no-one anywhere in this country can be isolated and feel themselves unconnected with anybody else if they are all going to vote. We have hammered home with our fifth and sixth formers the fact that they are making decisions and using their votes very soon – while still in school – in a way which will determine the fate of people elsewhere in this country. We wrote that into the first edition of our booklet and we have felt that it was very important ever since.

This is not even to do with the question whether one is

going to travel or take up a job somewhere else; but every time one exercises one's vote, one makes decisions for a vast number of people in this country and informs the policies of people who will be very powerful in determining their lives. This need not be just directly connected always with the issues in the booklet, but it is something that our fifth and sixth formers do not realise unless we are hammering it home all the time.

MS. BONNICK: May I refer back to the point that Peter Smith asked Winston? I feel that the debate which has been generated round the issue of separate schools is inadequately presented in the booklet, because I think that they are referred to as an esoteric response to culture and cultural maintenance. The real issues which have led especially the Afro-Caribbean community towards separate schools are the outcome of education – what happens, how do you evaluate and measure 11 years of schooling in terms of what students achieve at the end? Those issues should have been addressed in the booklet.

When we talk about teachers critically reflecting on their own practice, as teachers we also have to reflect particularly on the outcome of our teaching, and we have to take some responsibility for it. It is always quite easy for teachers to accept the successes, but they are never willing to accept the failures. We talk about failures and then we go back into pathological models of our families and so on and the different cultural predispositions of certain groups to take advantage of the education system; and we do not implicate ourselves in failure.

MR. SMITH: Just so that I understand the point clearly, would another way of making the point have been to say that not a clear enough connection is made between ethnic monitoring, monitoring and teaching practice?

MS. BONNICK: Yes, and also the pedagogy is crucial here. Even on the research side of the whole multi-cultural debate, we have not actually looked in any positive and critical way at the pedagogical practices of supplementary schools – the declared intention of those teachers when they go there, their defined jobs. Those things are transmitted very clearly to the kids who go there and they know why they are there. I would like us to look at what goes on in those schools and what bridges could be built between supplementary schools and mainstream schools. Some of the practices in those schools are very positive, some of which parents themselves would want to bring back into the mainstream school. To answer the point in another way, we must also talk about content.

MRS. SAM-BAILEY: I think that Peter Smith has raised a question similar to one that I wanted to ask. We do not see separate schools as an answer to the problem. Children have a right to education within the main stream and not separate. After all, when they leave school, they will have to work in this country with everybody else, so taking them away and educating them separately is not really preparing them for a place in society.

Some supplementary schools do a good job of helping the children to make up for what they have lost in the mainstream schools. Others, I am afraid, are not doing that. In fact, I know of supplementary schools which are engaged in indoctrination and Africanisation. I do not see that as serving the needs of the children.

MS. BONNICK: I always get concerned when people from ethnic minorities themselves talk about anything that they might do themselves as somehow not preparing children to live in this society. After all, we came here as people from the outside, and we made the adjustment. I do not think that a school – not that I am putting the case – designed to educate children in a different intellectual milieu is incapable of preparing them for their rightful place or function in British society.

My reference to the supplementary schools was based on the fact that it is true that we do not know generally what goes on in those schools to any great depth, because very little work has been done on them. However, the little that is available suggests that the approach to pedagogy is quite different in some instances from what takes place in mainstream schools – the fact that there is a kind of correspondence between the expectation of parents and the school; there is not that conflict. Those are the sort of issues that we have to address.

MR. MANYAN: As part of a supplementary school – the Robert Hardman, in Peckham – I would extend an invitation to anyone who wants to come and see us in operation to do so either one afternoon or on a statutory half-day. In my capacity as a pastoral leader, I have seen all outcomes in a positive perspective. Not all the production can be measured as such; there are no instruments for measuring it. Any good work that I do is shown when my pupils leave me and enter society at large, taking their different qualities with them. That is why I did not take that on board. I still find the report very comprehensive.

DR. STEVENS: May I say something about separate schools rather than supplementary schools? I completely agree that, where there are supplementary schools, there should be better contact, liaison and so on with the mainstream school. We say that somewhere in the report. What worries me is the separate schools – not the movement among some Afro-Caribbean parents who see this as a route to better achievement for their children, but what we see in some of the Asian schools in this country, where what they want is cultural separatism. There are some in existence as independent schools, small and under-funded, instilling a ghetto-like mentality.

The Working Party thinks that this is a move in entirely the wrong direction. If there is a place for separate schools – we do not come down on one side or the other of the argument; we see both sides – we believe that those separate schools should have exactly the same multi-cultural perspective in their curriculum as we advocate for the mainstream schools. It should happen in State schools, Church of England schools, Roman Catholic schools, and Moslem schools – everywhere.

Obviously, where a school is funded by a particular community, its perspective will of course focus from the position of that community – that is right and proper – but we believe that the right perspective has to be there. Our central concern is that these young people should have the choice of their future lifestyle. This is the central argument: mono-cultural ghetto schools – whether white and English or of any other kind – are working against that.

MR. THOMPSON: Not all of us on the working party are in favour of the present system of separate voluntary-aided schools. As one who works in such a school, I would love to see them all abolished and made into mainstream schools. This does not mean that we would be opposed to an independent type of school for people who want some separation, but again it should have a multi-cultural context in what it provides.

On supplementary schools, I am afraid of people who talk about "Africanisation." I know that the word has a political overtone in many cases which we do not accept, but it can be understood in another way. The word does not fall easily from the lips, but I cannot see any harm in "Polishisation," by means of which the great grandchildren of Polish immigrants are learning Polish language and culture. Another example is "Ukrainianisation"; not only does it have such objectives, but it attempts to persuade its children to celebrate Christmas at the wrong time, and is doing so successfully. I have no objection to that. The supplementary schools which are fulfilling that function and maintaining part of the cultural diversity are doing something that we applaud. If it has political overtones, we do not like it.

But to come back to what may not be in our document and perhaps should be, I should like to put it in the context of how it has come to my mind. I have recently read the report of an HMI inspection lasting a week of one department in a school. The things that the inspectors commended are a rather interesting cross-section when related to the staff concerned, because in that department, half the lessons are taught by teachers who for one reason or another teach half a timetable or thereabouts. It is the work of those teachers that has, indirectly, been commended. I believe that this could be pulled out of the report and attention drawn to it. The teachers whose lessons were best prepared and who did the best

161

assessment of work were, if you like, the part-timers. The inspectors did not put it so bluntly, but reading between the lines, one can see a lot of truth in it.

I started teaching bright boys chemistry. The diversity has increased each year until it is now almost unbelievable – not only boys and girls in the same classes, which is a marked improvement, but mixed ability, special needs, cultural diversity and so on. We have to widen the areas that our subjects cover, so as to cover a wider section of society. All this diversity has to be accommodated in our lessons. This is easier in smaller classes than larger ones. It was very significant that the only two adverse reports from the HMI team were on classes which were over-sized. So the size of classes has something to do with all this.

There is also a time factor. There is a need for teachers to co-ordinate with all sorts of demands and organisations – not just the multi-cultural input, but the feeder schools, the local FE establishments, the ethnic groups, the supplementary schools, not to mention the police. All those things are being raised by this Association. As the PTA has grown up in a way that did not exist before, that is another thing that takes more time.

One reaches the limit. One reads the documents from the DES: that about science suggests what primary teachers should do. If they could have another three hours per day or another day per week, they could fit it all in and do it well. We need more man hours and woman hours to get this work done. Multi-cultural and anti-racist education is part of the workload that teachers are taking upon themselves and which is now also being imposed on them by the authorities. This all requires resourcing in terms of manpower. More teachers are needed to do it.

As for the word "directive" – the anti-racist directive on FE – it reminds me that somebody said, "If you throw a bottle of scent at a lady, she will not like the perfume." Throwing money and then issuing directives on other matters will not be as acceptable as the sum of money that one wants from the

Secretary of State. Directives and imposed settlements are along the same lines: you need an incentive to be able to do it.

Mike Stevens spoke about the teachers themselves producing the resources in the climate to produce multi-cultural and anti-racist education in response to the demand. As he said, the difficulty is in the suburban areas. A recent television programme showed children living in such an area less than ten minutes bus ride from the ethnic area of Leicester. The teachers in that area have no incentive in the school to produce this approach. I am afraid that the directives from on high telling them that they must do it will not succeed; but when the recommended curriculum or the syllabus or the text book or the video programme or whatever resources they use include the ethnic diversity angle automatically, then they will begin to see its benefit. That is the incentive: "This is a good idea; we will adapt it and use it."

MR. SMITH: I wanted to come back to Lemah's point about the issues which seem to her to be very difficult. I hope that I may be permitted to import a problem that I came across. I was not involved in writing or drafting this booklet at all, but the same committee that set up this Working Party set up another to look at the implications of the sex education clause in the 1986 Act. Originally, we wanted to produce a brief guide to the law as we understood it, but that publication has taken off.

When doing that drafting, I came across an issue which is in a subsection headed "The role of women", which potentially gets one into considerable problems. Whether we have been able to get ourselves out of them, I do not know, but perhaps I could quote the rather Delphic sentences on this topic:

> "Most teachers will readily accept that it is undesirable for them to deal with sex education in a way which seems to set out to imply criticism of parents' attitudes. It is equally important, however, that teachers should seek to promote mutual respect and equality between the sexes. AMMA considers that it is an entirely appropriate educational objective to teach adolescent girls and

163

their male peers that they are more than potentially subservient child bearers and rearers. Pursuit of that objective, however tactful and sensitive, may, in the case of some cultural groups, run strongly counter to the mores, convictions and expectations of their parents."

In a sense, we neatly flunk out of the argument by saying that, in the society we have, teachers will be presented with a dilemma.

The question then arises in the context of this discussion and the other discussion: is it a soluble dilemma or not?

MS. BONNICK: I think it would be soluble for some groups. Some groups of parents would take on the teaching of sex education outside the framework of family and marriage and so forth, and other groups would not. Even within your own society there are parents who believe – we had a directive from the DES or a statement to this effect – that sex education should be taught within the framework of marriage. So even that statement itself is not contradictory as between the dominant group and some minority cultures. There are different groups of people who would accept it.

MR. SMITH: But the groups where it is not acceptable are the real dilemma, it seems to me – where ethnic and cultural identity and religious conviction are powerfully intertwined.

MR. MANYAN: Those small groups would have to rethink their religious or ideological beliefs in the light of this new dimension to health education. It is all changing in the present climate I dare say that they will rethink.

MS. BONNICK: I should like to come back to some of the points about the whole notion of what forms of separation are acceptable and what forms are not. I feel – I do not know whether this is a cop out – that if you claim that we live in a plural society, we have to accept that some of the plurality will be unacceptable to some us. There is no uniformity. We had to accept, under the 1944 Education Act, that some groups, for religious reasons, believe so strongly in the religious component of secular life that there is no distinction, and they want education to reflect that. We have had to accept that with Jewish schools and so on, and we have co-existed with them reasonably well.

I do not feel so threatened personally by the idea that the Afro-Caribbean groups with specific views and philosophies of education would wish to set up their own schools – or by the idea of separate education for girls and so on. I do not feel that such notions of separateness prevents us from bringing debates within the kind of separate groups that we have now.

MR. THOMPSON: I have a feeling about the extreme groups with extreme views on religion or education who wish to set up completely independent establishments for that purpose; they are not the kind of people who then say that, as a result of that separation, they are disadvantaged and that therefore society is against them. They accept that, as one of the constraints which they willingly bear because they have given a high priority to these other things. But I get concerned when such a group can run an establishment with a wider recruitment than its own members and then can start imposing its ideas upon people who have not subscribed to the entire ethos and are not basically prepared to make the sacrifices which are needed to put into practice those extreme views. They then feel a sense of deprivation, and – possibly justifiably – they feel isolated.

DR. STEVENS: Even then, when some groups are taking this decision to make this sacrifice, they are not making the sacrifice just on their own behalf but on behalf of their children – by committing their children to an educational establishment designed to shut them in and limit their opportunities. It is not their sacrifice, but their children's sacrifice: that is what worries me.

MISS GRAY: I was trying to find the reference which caused a tremendous amount of heart-searching in our first version of the pamphlet, at the beginning of the series. On page 7, we were going through the debate, and at that time it was mainly in connection with the idea of assimilation or not. We came down in the end with the idea that the worst circumstances were those in which, in ordinary schools, one was aware of the stance of parents who would not be entirely happy if teachers were trying, in the most respectable way possible, to give the young people choices based on different attitudes to life and different sorts of customs and so on, which we thought that every child growing up should have. We came down in the end on the point that we thought that the boys and girls must be given the knowledge and the choice. We had to open up that possibility for them, even when we felt that we might be running counter to some extent to the attitude of some of the parents. You had to show respect to the family attitudes, but you had to say, "This is what we believe it is right for us to do for these children, to give them the opportunity to make their own choices as they grow up." Some of those issues later on have involved us in following this through, where we had to say, "This is where we stand and you will have to know about our stand. It may be different from your parents' and you will make the ultimate choice for yourselves."

It comes back to the point that we have found extraordinarily difficult. The attitudes of teachers while they are doing that and taking that line, must be so very sensitive.

MS. BONNICK: In the last ten years or so, a significant amount of research has suggested that girls do better in all-girls schools. The reason why some would argue this is that, when they are on their own and not with boys, teachers cannot marginalise the girls; they have to give them the curriculum in its entirety. They cannot say, "This is masculine and that is feminine." We operate on the notion that, even in co-educational schools, girls are given this choice. We know that it is not a simple, straightforward choice but is mediated by many other complex factors.

Many people who have put forward that reasoning have now begun to re-evaluate it: under what conditions can I optimise my child's choice in a society that I know is fundamentally unequal? If I, for example, live in a racist society, is it better for me, knowing that racism operates, even in a school where teachers are fighting to remove racism and optimise my child's choice, to ask what impact that would have on my child? Would it not be better for my child to be in a school where that negotiation is not taking place, where certain things are taken for granted? I have chosen my pressure; I have decided that there are certain pressures which are perhaps more crucial and which will have much more impact in the long term than others. I might decide to concentrate on giving my child this, knowing that I might be short-changing the child in another direction, but that it is possible to take corrective measures in that respect later on, in a way that I cannot for something else.

MS. KLEIN: I wanted to try to answer this question a little. The document is too good to go down the drain. I have a couple of little points that I want to pick up, but I would do that with individual members.

However, there is a major issue here, which is beginning to be felt. Teachers are service providers. We are inclined to ask: should we tell parents what they should want for their children, or should we listen to parents? It is my view of education that, if children are educated to have the confidence in themselves and their learning skills, they could learn in a fairly narrow framework of a body of knowledge and then extend themselves into the wider area should they so choose. So there is no reason why children should not have a separatist education if they can acquire those skills and that confidence. They could then acquire all that they needed for a doctorate at Cambridge – although that is a narrow field. They could narrow or widen as they chose. The separatist option needs to be indicated, but it is not for AMMA or any body of teachers or any one provider to take what the position might be. It is the service provision which is not adequately addressed in this document.

Nor must we forget the research orientation, which is indeed another cop-out. Far too much research is into the pupils and far too little into the teachers. I would have liked more attention paid and more comment made and recommendations supported by research. That includes the report that the DES was so unhappy with on the career and vocational opportunities of ethnic minority young people aged 15 to 18. It was a polite report, in DES-funded terminology, which, according to much of the press – including the Daily Telegraph – the Department did its damndest to lose and to flush out, with no release and no press embargo. One wonders whether there was a conspiracy, and one tends to think there was. The report has now come out privately as "Education for Some" and it is known as the Eggleston report.

That was a much more sustained and apparently authoritative body of research which considered teacher practice and behaviour and which picked up something which was tucked away in annex 20, chapter 2, of the Swann report – including the interaction between boys and girls, black, Indian, Asian and white, and how they were treated by teachers in one classroom.

That has now been extended to wider issues – not just what goes on in each classroom but what goes on in each school with banding, allocation of exam sets, the ethos in the school, the counter-measures the pupils take, and so on. There was also the ethnographic study fitted into that report, which is one reason why nobody wanted it too widely disseminated.

Cecile Wright's ethnographic study of Afro-Caribbean children and how they are treated in two schools in a Midlands shire county has begun to describe the phenomenon of black kids coming in with a rather higher reading age than the average for their year. By the third year, not only are they significantly dropping back, but they are moving around the school together. That must create terror and a battleground situation in the school, but why has it happened? What are the children trying to tell us? What is going on in the classroom? Cecile answers that to some extent with overt incidents, such as that of child coming into a class late and, in front of the rest of the class, being told, "If you are not careful, I will send you back to the chocolate factory to be made over." Other staff have admitted that that is something that that teacher has been known to say more than once. This seminal research is vital and it puts this issue where it should be – which is why it is needed.

Teachers are service providers. I hope that AMMA will do more than produce this document, that it will put some professional weight behind it, to demand of its members that they see it as part of their professionalism to consider very carefully how they are behaving in the schools, what they are saying in the all-white schools when there is graffiti outside saying, "Pakis go home" and nobody bothers to remove it. That is where more emphasis needs to be put.

MR. SMITH: I am not dissenting from any of Gillian's comments, but I want to marry some of the things she said with what Lemah Bonnick said. In the end, I come closer than I would wish to do to thinking that their observations are in a sense a cop-out, as they feared they might be.

If you take the view that the education service is indeed a service industry, for want of a better word, and if you say that it is a national service, although locally delivered, which has to assume that all consumers are entitled to take advantage of it and to find in it that which will meet their expectations, you should not base the national education service on a sort of "like it or lump it" philosophy, in which, if your lumping it is powerfully enough felt, you will set up your own school.

If you start on that basis, I continue to have great difficulty in reconciling – I do not want to narrow it to the single issue of sex education – conflicting and equally held social priorities, which are not merely social priorities but legally reinforced. We have on the one hand the Race Relations Act and on the other hand the Sex Discrimination Act. That was certainly in my mind over that issue, but I would not want to narrow it to that.

It seems to me more general – that the inherent, inescapable, inevitable downside of the diversity of a multi-cultural society is that there always will be tensions which come from the diversity itself. I think that if you try to write yourself out of those tensions, smooth them over, you are copping out of an important argument.

For example, to come right back to language, there has to be a tension between teaching children to speak or write in registers which are useful, acceptable and advantageous for the purposes of everyday life and allotting the cultural respect and primacy that one should to the culture from which they were derived. I have a feeling that in the end an attempt to find a linguistic or philosophical solution to that puzzle is in a way a kind of escapism from the official argument.

MRS. BROWN: I felt my defensiveness coming to the fore slightly when Mrs. Klein was speaking. I wanted to defend our document. We were recalled, as it were, to respond to Swann, and out of Swann, we then widened our focus, knowing that there was so much that we could do; but we also had to remember that we were all practising teachers, with our marking to do in the evening and our reading to keep up with on topical matters. Our working week tends to be 80 or 90 hours, let alone all the other developments we should be keeping track of. For me, that meant a great deal of midnight oil, reading even the things that Mrs. Klein wrote.

Another point which should be aired is not given a lot of room in our document. I need here to be slightly anecdotal. My husband and I are very culturally diverse, but we get along –

MS. BONNICK: That is in the nature of marriage.

MRS. BROWN: Yes. In the six years that I have been on this Working Party, naturally we have had a lot of discussion about the multi-cultural scene. I would say that my husband began, as a great jazz lover, being much more aware of multi-cultural aspects than I, but we seem since to have swung around a bit, until he veers towards integration and he is now beginning to feel threatened by the various pressure groups which say that he should think this way or that he should not think that way.

In common with many other people, he has somewhat lost his way. Not being able to read and have access to the documents that we as teachers and educationalists see, he cannot make up for it in quite the same way as we say that we practising teachers should be doing.

MS. KLEIN: I have to respond, because what I said was not an attack. There seems to be a strategy in this kind of debate, where people say, "I think this is very good, but" – and then go for the jugular. That is not what I did. I was sincere in saying that this is a very good document and that what I can do to publicise it I shall do – as I did with the first one. Vast quantities of it went through my hands and it was probably heard about as a result.

What I am really saying is that teacher practice needs to be far more carefully challenged. While I commend the Association for putting the word "anti-racist" on the cover and finding it advisable to mention why, it is not enough just to have it on the cover. I would like to see that that is what you are really talking about. Teachers' behaviour is sometimes, very occasionally overtly racist, as in the example I quoted. Rampton used the phrase "unintentionally racist", which has been critised as letting people off the hook. We have to make teachers aware of ways in which they are covertly or unintentionally racist. They need to be told that that is not on, that it will do no-one any good. I am not confident that that is strongly enough articulated throughout your booklet.

Dorritt McAuslan once said that she came from a group which had been most researched into – "and we don't like it."

Teachers need to be researched into. Any such document today, even taking Swann as its starting point, needs to address that point very carefully. These issues of equality tell us something about the overall ethos and value system and ideals – philosophy of education – which look at issues of gender equality, class equality and certainly equality of ethnic minorities, against the background of racism and discrimination in our society. That needs to be built into the practice of all teachers and the research that they should be providing in schools. We need to make teachers more aware that they are not yet doing this and that to a large extent, however unintentionally, they are doing the opposite. That is what I am really worried about – that you do a great deal, but not quite enough.

MRS. WHITELEY: Do you not consider these words on page 104 strong enough:

"This does require a considerable level of individual and group self-awareness."?

That is why I was talking about a half-day, which I meant not as a one-off but as an introduction to any external INSET, so that staff could discuss things among themselves. They will not do it if there is an outside speaker, with everybody in the hall.

MISS GRAY: This was very much in our minds. We are not lacking in very strong conviction, but we were beginning to encounter those who found it too easy to dismiss some of these questions if they thought that we were coming with a slogan. We were trying to get away from the sort of phrases that they were familiar with, and perhaps we have understated the case because of that. That was very much in our minds in the document.

DR. STEVENS: We were aware that one thing that we were trying to do was offer some leadership to our members. It is a mistake to try to lead too quickly, because you will not be followed.

MS. KLEIN: Yes, and slaps on the wrist will not help either. But there are children in the schools now who need help.

I would not change a word of the document; I would only say that if you orientate more of the work around in the inequalities and inadequacies of teacher practice which are emerging from research which is documented time and again in the TES, that is something which should be more clearly emphasised.

MR. THOMPSON: Is the remedy to the problem so neatly described by Gillian another chapter rather than an alteration to any of the existing chapters?

MS. KLEIN: I would hate to see you have to rewrite this.

MR. THOMPSON: When Ms. Klein was speaking, Gillian's first response was that to some extent we must accept that the chapters in this booklet are largely determined by the people who were on the Working Party. I can imagine that, if somebody different had been on the Working Party, there would have been an entirely different chapter covering an entirely different aspect of the problem. Perhaps, if someone else had been on the Working Party, a whole chapter would have been devoted to the problem that Ms. Klein has in mind, rather than trying to modify any existing chapter to cover the topic or to deal with the problem.

MR. MANYAN: When I speak, I feel that I speak as an AMMA member, although I am actually NUT. I wanted to defend the document as well, but I did not think that it was my job. I agree with the need for more investigation into teachers' behaviour, but the climate was inappropriate, in the light of what has been happening with teachers over the last two years, to launch what would have been seen as another attack. It is speaking very frankly to expose this kind of behaviour, which is unintentional. Those concerned are not aware of it – at least, we must go on that assumption. Perhaps an annex dealing separately with these issues might be useful.

MR. SMITH: As you know, a note is being taken of this conversation, and Gillian's comments will be reproduced fully. But that is too easy a way of disposing of the point, which I do not think should be disposed of. In addition to what Winston has just said, which I wholeheartedly endorse, it would have been precisely the wrong time at any moment in the last two years – and it is still the wrong moment now – to turn to our own members, whom we are defending against criticisms that we believe are unwarranted, and say, "Actually, we have a few criticisms of our own." There might have been a sharp reaction to that.

That leads me on to perhaps a slightly different point. In a way, following what Winston said, unions are always in that kind of fix, I think. As Mike Stevens said, sometimes you skin a cat very slowly: it is more painful, but you get the fur off in one piece.

But the serious question is this: where is the start point for the initiative which is needed? Does it come from teachers' unions or organisations exhorting their members with considerable frankness, or does it come – to get us into another very slippery argument – from local authorities explicitly and overtly articulating detailed policy – not just pious thoughts but policy in terms of practice and the consequences of mal-practice, and standing the flak of the undoubted media mis-interpretation which that will attract?

MS. KLEIN: That is why I would like to see more research. I would like it to stem from the research.

MS. BONNICK: But after the research, there is still the problem of implementation. This is where the point arises of the local authorities, and getting teaching staff to get the sanction from their unions. This represents the triple approach which is necessary, but it is not an approach without difficulties. The recent events in Brent have demonstrated that the triple approach did not work out too well there.

MR. MANYAN: Yes, I was about to suggest that the initial point should be from the local authorities, the politicians.

MS. KLEIN: There are 33 or 34 local authorities with multi-cultural or anti-racist education policies, and that is not enough. It will not go far enough. That poor old cat will be naked sooner or later. Change is painful, it is an amenable struggle, and it will be hard. This is the reality. AMMA has, I think, handled things better than a lot of people would. Your first document was almost as painless as anything advocating change could be, and I was gratified to see the responses to it. What you are doing is extremely valuable, but there is still far too much emphasis on research into "these black kids" and not enough into "that education system" or "those teachers".

Again, if you want to start talking about best practice, instead of researching these highly achieving black children, let us look at those highly achieving teachers. That is fairly well documented, so you have researched some of the teacher work. Perhaps you need to show some other aspects.

THE CHAIRMAN: Mr. Stratton, quite a time ago, you said that you had one or two comments that you wanted to make.

MR. STRATTON: I feel that I am listening rather than contributing. The problem for us in teacher training is that it all comes down to how we implement some of the ideas. The problem, of course, is clear: we have three different bands – the people who are coming in the first time for initial teacher training; those on postgraduate training; and those doing in-service training. As you were talking, I was thinking of some way of congealing these ideas into a common syllabus, but I am afraid that I cannot think of a common thread.

My principal interest is linguistics and language, and I think that it would be a presumption to impose that emphasis on any document as a response to the needs, as we see them, of teacher training. If we took, with the initial teacher training, something like language awareness as the keynote area, again that is documented in your publication. If, for the post-graduate people, we took the body of knowledge approach rather than an attitudinal approach, then you have the major problem of which approach to language ascription you use. We have not solved this one. For instance, you have the psychological or social-analytical approaches to the problem of initial trainees, but postgraduates, with an assumed body of knowledge, are already further on than initial training people.

For the in-service people, it would be something to do with starting from practice, from what goes on in the schools. Again this area has not been resolved clearly enough in your document, but there is a major problem here: how do we analyse the empirical situations in the classroom and convince teachers that there is one particular approach to adopt as a solution to the first point that I mentioned, which is either an attitudinal change or behavioural change?

There is a chronology there, of bringing about some behavioural change in training, but you have to change attitudes first. How do you do this? Is it absorbed knowledge, a body of knowledge that we talk about, or is it an eclectic thing relating to syllabus content areas?

As I see it, you have raised very interesting points, but I do not have any answers about implementation, except that we would have to come up with some curriculum response, some content area at the training college end which we would try to implement for all teachers in training. How we do this is up to us, because we have the privilege of devising our own syllabus. We can do virtually what we like, if we come up with a course which is approved by the university. We have tremendous freedom within those two structures, so I suppose that it is up to us to try to approach all teacher trainees, whether initial, post-graduate or in-service, to convince them that an attitudinal change is needed in the way in which we have to try to implement, so that they will try to change their teaching behaviour, eventually.

That is how I see it, but it is a diverse response because it is a diffuse matter.

MR. BEASTALL: I have one point of substance and one minor matter to raise. The first is the use of the term "anti-racist". I know that this is a very difficult area. One of the good things about your document is the fact that, at the beginning, you talk about "racism" and what it means and so on.

Just so that you know, in Government circles, the use of the term "anti-racist" is not encouraged, simple because it is ambiguous. It is used in different senses by different people. It can mean opposition to racism and the methods to that end, which is a very acceptable usage. But in some circles, it has ideological connotations which can switch people off when they hear the word mentioned.

It is not for me to suggest what the title of your document should be, but I slightly worried about the fact that that word appears in the title, which might mean that some people would not read it who otherwise would and would thus benefit from it. Perhaps an alternative might be "anti-discriminatory" or something like that.

On a totally different point, and one of detail, the second chapter from the end talks about the collection and use of statistics. It does not actually mention the fact that the Secretary of State, last July when he accepted the Working Party's recommendations, also said that he proposed to go for a system of national aggregation – and I know that it is AMMA's view that it would be appropriate to do that. I hope that, when we produce the draft circular, it will be clear how we propose to approach that. That might be worth a comment.

DR. STEVENS: I thank everybody very much indeed for their contributions, which will make a very interesting postscript to our document. As Gillian Klein and other people have said, It has set the agenda to a considerable extent for what comes next – for AMMA and other people as well.

THE CHAIRMAN: I reiterate those words. This discussion has given AMMA a professional challenge, to put some weight behind the document and to disseminate it to all our members, north and south, east and west, remembering above all the importance of the classroom teacher and the fact that things begin in the classroom. It is on that that we must build, looking more closely at initial training and in-service programmes – what they have done and how they fit the needs of what we are trying to do, against the background of this document. We must also try to negotiate some more time in which we may do some of this training, so that we are not just living off our own humps, as we have been doing for so long.

We must be looking at good practice, including cascade systems – in fact, doing all we can not only to give information to our members but also to feed the classroom teachers, our colleagues in school, with any substance that we can find that will help them in the years ahead when they are looking at cross-curricular activities against the background of a document such as this.

Change and challenge are ever-present. One sometimes in school wishes for a moment of consolidation, but it would seem to me that that is a faint hope at the moment. We do need to take this document very seriously indeed, and to note very carefully the postscript or appendix to it. On that note, I thank you all very much for your attendance and your contributions.

The Seminar closed at 12.15 p.m.

Appendix 5

Anti-racist education in the 1990s

Since the publication of *Multi-Cultural and Anti-Racist Education Today* in December 1987, there has been intense public debate arising from a few well-publicised incidents in which anti-racist education has been seen, rightly or wrongly, as a factor. The Macdonald report (unpublished but extensively leaked) on the murder of an Asian pupil at Burnage High School Manchester, various disputes about culturally mixed schools in Bradford, the ILEA's actions over Highbury Quadrant Primary School and the Salman Rushdie affair have all led some writers to attack the notion of anti-racist policies in schools, and of anti-racist and multi-cultural education generally. In this context we feel it appropriate to publish supplementary advice to members.

We believe that the principles expressed in the book still hold good. Our society, whether viewed nationally or internationally, is inherently multi-cultural and this inescapable fact needs to be acknowledged within the curriculum and organisation of any educational institution. Furthermore, the existence of widespread racism, institutional and unrealised as well as individual and overt, is also a fact that must be addressed. To the extent that education needs to work for a better, more just society, (and we believe that it should), then its aims should include the promotion of cross-cultural understanding and the discouragement of prejudice. To the extent that some individuals in our education system are handicapped by racism in society, and we believe that many are, then the education service can be properly effective for them only if it contains elements whose purpose is to offset that handicap. We believe that these two elements in education are not optional extras that can be grafted on to the main stem but are themselves an integral part of what constitutes a good education in the present context. For several years the need for a multi-cultural approach to the curriculum has been a constant theme in pronouncements from HMI, the DES and Parliament.

Having said that, we believe it is necessary to respond in a subtle way to the recent debates and to the backlash against the concept of anti-racist education. There are some groups who promulgate approaches to racism based more on revenge for past ills than on the avoidance of future ones. We reject such views as vehemently as we do those which pretend that racism does not exist or can be ignored. It is unfortunate that strident argument between supporters of these opposing camps has badly clouded the public debate. What matters are the ideas, as expressed in the previous paragraph. It may be that these ideas can best be expedited in the immediate future if the controversial phrase 'anti-racist' is avoided. Perhaps the ideas can more usefully be expressed in terms of equality of opportunity. But they do need to be expressed and to be put into practice. The incidents referred to above may make the choice of language for the debate harder, but we believe that they only sharpen the need for well-judged application of the principles to the everyday practice in schools and colleges.

Policy and practice in schools and colleges

For an institution to have a written anti-racist policy is not enough: if the policy is not well-judged, clearly defined and firmly realised in daily practice then it can have the opposite effect to that intended. The policy also needs to be well known to staff, students/pupils and the wider school/college community. It needs, for example, to be outlined in the literature sent to prospective pupils/students and their families and to feature significantly in the induction of new members of staff.

The whole curriculum needs a multi-cultural perspective in order that pupils and students learn to understand and respect people from different backgrounds from their own and to value diversity rather than fearing it. This is needed whether or not the school or college itself contains an ethnic diversity: it is most unlikely today that anyone will spend their whole life in a mono-cultural enclave within our multi-cultural society. The multi-cultural curriculum is discussed in some detail in *Multi-Cultural and Anti-Racist Education Today* Chapter 4. But this multi-culturalism needs to be approached in a way that recognises the common humanity of all ethnic groups and avoids driving wedges between them.

179

The curriculum also needs to give consideration to racism (and other forms of group prejudice) as a subject for study in its own right, so that on the one hand its supporters can be challenged and on the other its victims can understand what they face and prepare their mental defences. The approach will clearly need to be tailored to the age of the pupils concerned. To make it explicit may be inappropriate before the secondary phase of education. In that sector there are many different subject-headings under which it can be treated: History, RE and PSE are some of the more obvious examples. The school's policy should make sure that the topic is on the syllabus for all pupils at an appropriate age and that it doesn't fall into the gap where everyone believes that somebody else will see to it.

In addition to what is planned in the curriculum, all staff must be ready to address issues of racism as and when they are encountered in the classroom or elsewhere in the institution, by responding appropriately to pupils' comments and challenging negative attitudes and stereotypes. This is as relevant to what goes on in the staffroom as elsewhere. There will be times when it is necessary for those in leadership positions to make clear the principles on which they stand.

The institution's organisational procedures should be carefully studied and any accidentally discriminatory elements corrected. Such areas as uniform, meals and PE arrangements can be possible areas for unrealised discrimination which need to be checked and, where necessary, discussed carefully with parents and the community as indicated below.

The institution needs to have, and to make known, a set of routines to follow in the case of any racist incident. These need (i) to be graduated to deal with different levels of seriousness, (ii) to be known to and observed by all staff, (iii) to articulate with other routines and structures, and (iv) to have been devised and promulgated in a way that maximises their support and understanding in the school/college community as a whole.

The school or college also has to have agreed and widely-known ways of handling allegations of racism within its community, whether these allegations are made against students or staff. These procedures should avoid two dangers. Such allegations should not be trivialised. But there should be a very conscious effort on the part of those who have to respond to such complaints to avoid the trap of pre-judging them on the basis of the race of the complainant or of the accused. A working assumption that all white people are racist is no more and no less destructive than one that all black people "have a chip on their shoulder". Either is seriously offensive and unjust. But either can lurk, sometimes unrealised, in a corner of the mind even of someone who would firmly reject their more overt forms. Stringent self-analysis is essential for those whose duties involve examining allegations of racism.

The institution needs consciously to look out for the symptoms of racial tension in its own community or the wider community surrounding it. The reasons why this matters are described on pages 99 -100 of *Multi-Cultural and Anti-Racist Education Today* and some of the symptoms to look for are mentioned on pages 101 and 102. Specifically the dominance of racially based friendship groups can indicate the existence of racial tension in the minds of the pupils concerned. Even if the sources of such tension lie outside the school or college, they will inevitably affect relationships within it.A supportive attitude to students who are the victims of such external pressure is necessary if the school or college is not to be seen by such students as contributing to the pressure.

While the various procedures involved in dealing with racist incidents will need to vary considerably from one institution to another, we believe that there is one factor that should always be present. In *Multi-Cultural and Anti-Racist Education Today* we say (on page 102):

A policy that, following any racially motivated incident, the offender's parents are seen by senior staff produces a double benefit. Where school and parents agree about the unacceptable nature of the offence, they can work together. Where the parents themselves exhibit racial prejudice, to make the school's disapproval clear to them may not necessarily cause them to modify their views but will be an influence to moderate their expression of those views.

We believe that what we said in 1987 is still important today, especially in the context we shall describe in section 3 below.

Developing the policy

The development of such a policy and of the practices which follow from it needs to take place in a way that fosters a sense of ownership of the policy and practice by the whole of the school or college community. This is almost certainly best achieved by opening up the process of policymaking to participation by all sections of the school or college community. If this is done, then the process of formulating the policy will itself be a valuable contribution to mutual understanding between the different community groups. The process can be almost as important as the resulting policy.

There need to be major inputs to such policy-making not only from teaching staff, but from support staff, pupils/students, their families and relevant community groups. Where there is a PTA, it ought to be involved, and to be persuaded to consider just how representative it is of the school's wider community. Governing bodies need to be explicitly involved. LEA guidelines may exist, and may be helpful (not only in the LEA's own schools). If the former is true but not the latter, then the school or college may wish to raise the matter with the LEA.

No ethnic group should be given any reason to feel excluded from this process. While there is certainly a place for specific input to the process from individual ethnic groups, it is just as important that the main arenas for discussion cut across ethnic divisions, in order that the different groups can feel that they are working together to understand one another's problems and to find mutual solutions. In that way a widely-held consensus of support for the resulting policies is most likely to be achieved.

It is important that the policy, and the discussion that leads to it, are based on realistic ideas of what the world is like. There are, for example, particular dangers in assuming that somebody's attitude to other ethnic groups can be deduced from the colour of their skin. We believe that the wider the range of people involved in the debate, the better chance there will be of avoiding sterile theoretical approaches.

While wide discussion of future policy is important, it should not be allowed unreasonably to defer implementation of what is agreed at an early stage. There is an argument for the gradual introduction of policies as sections of them are agreed. There are also pitfalls to be wary of. To introduce a system, for example, for reporting incidents is likely to produce only frustration and tension if there are no procedures in place to respond to incidents so reported. Nevertheless, there can be a place (and there is often a need) for interim policies and practices to be put in place while more satisfactory ones are still in the planning stage.

Once the policy is agreed and in place, it needs to be reviewed regularly to ensure that the procedures are working as intended, and that both policy and practice keep abreast of changing circumstances.

The right context

When highly-charged incidents take place in a school or college, whatever their origin, then many parts of the institution's practice are put under stress. Since racism, real or alleged, is an issue full of high emotional charge, then institutions need protection against the damage that can come from a crisis centred on alleged or actual racism. By far the best form of such protection is for all the institution's policies and practices (not only those concerning racism) to be well-conceived and confidently adhered to.

Good communications are an obvious prerequisite, not only within the teaching staff but between all parts of the school or college community, and with the wider community outside. The necessity of inducting new staff into the procedures for dealing with racist incidents and allegations has already been mentioned. This needs to be part of a wider policy on the induction of new teachers, support staff and students.

We have discussed above the need to involve the school/college community (in the widest sense of that phrase) in the development of policies on equality of opportunity and racist pressures and incidents. This is considerably facilitated if such an approach to policy-making in general is already part of the system. If the areas we discuss here are the first upon which the institution seeks a wider community involvement in determining policy, there is likely to be pressure for similar approaches to extend to other parts of the school or college's policy and practice.

It is vital that teaching and support staff keep abreast of the concerns and fears of their pupils/students. This is the main way in which they can learn of good and bad developments within the community. Not only must they be alert to notice what such concerns are, but they need to believe that students' concerns really do matter to the health of the school or college as a community.

There is great danger in sudden over-reaction to a perceived crisis. Policies and procedures that are well-known and genuinely supported (in practice as well as on paper) are probably the best way of avoiding this. An institutional style based on calm responses is also of great use in helping ensure that reactions to potential crises are well-judged.

Violence and harassment within the school or college community are separate issues from that of anti-racism. Both or them can exist with or without racist intent or implications. But unless the institution has a sound and workable approach to violence and harassment, it is unlikely to respond in a well-judged manner to any specifically racial manifestations of them within or outside its walls.